D1584625

WORDS
of my father

a selection of talks written
and broadcast by the late
Rev. James L. Dow

Compiled by his son, Tom

OTHER BOOKS BY JAMES L. DOW

No Better Than I Should Be (Autobiography)
Graham Came by Cleish
Late and Early
A Dictionary of the Bible
American Wit and Wisdom
A History of Greenock

Published by Whitewisp Press
13 The Ness, Dollar, Clackmannanshire FK14 7EB
e-mail: whitewisppress@lineone.net

Typeset in Garamond 11/13

Printed in Scotland by Gardner Gibson Print Ltd, Renfrew

ISBN 0-9540217-0-3

FOREWORD

by the Rev. Douglas Aitken
formerly Senior Radio Producer, Religious Broadcasting, BBC Scotland

JIMMY Dow was a man of words. In Scots or English, he always chose the perfect word to say what he wanted to say with power. I had the privilege of being his radio producer on a number of occasions, both in the BBC studios in Glasgow and on an outside broadcast in St Bride's Church, Lochranza, Isle of Arran, his last parish.

He was always a joy to work with – keen to get things absolutely right, yet full of fun and laughter. Always his aim was to share his faith in the living God. His greatest wish was that people should not see his God as a distant, unreachable spirit, but a power for ordinary living in the every day. God was for the people and it was Jimmy's rich Scots brogue and gravelly voice that demanded that you listened and took note and believed that the God of everything was your God too, whoever you were. I can still hear it.

So it was with a little apprehension that I started to read the manuscript of this book. I know from long experience that what I write on paper, I speak better. How would words written for speaking look on the printed page? I'll tell you, I simply could not put the manuscript down.

Yes, of course I could hear that wonderful voice but even if I couldn't, his words would have been compelling reading. For in these pages Tom Dow has gathered words of his father that are for young and old, rich and poor, for everyone. I am glad he has done this for they will bring a tear to the eye, a smile to the lips, a laugh that shakes the body and a thought that shakes the soul.

This should be required reading for students of communication and students of life, for kings and commoners, for preachers and politicians and for you and me.

I wish this book well and hope that many will read it and enjoy it as much as I have.

CONTENTS

INTRODUCTION

WHEN my father died in 1977 my mother, my sister Margaret and I had the daunting task of trying to put into some kind of order the mass of paper he had generated over the years in the way of sermons, plays, books and scripts.

I decided I would like to keep as many scripts and sermons as I could find, but only typed versions as my father's writing although very neat was small and extremely difficult to read. I always joked with him that the only person who could read it was possibly the chemist.

My idea was that evenually I would try to publish some of these along the lines of his book *Late and Early* which was published in 1972. After reading this book again I decided that a combination of the contents of this book and some unpublished material might be worth producing.

In Thought for the Day (1) you will see a reference to Rev. Douglas Aitken who produced several of my father's broadcasts for the BBC. Douglas has now retired to Saline, and on making contact with him I was greatly encouraged by his interest and advice. Douglas provided the mising link in my files by finding a copy of Thought for the Day (2) in his loft. I would also like to thank Douglas for writing the foreword to the book.

To my wife Eilidh, a special word of thanks for her patience and encouragement during the many hours of work producing this book, and to Shania Twain, Nanci Griffith and Classic FM for providing background music. I would also like to thank my friend Albert Tonner for designing the cover.

I hope you enjoy reading it as much as I did compiling it.

Tom Dow
Dollar
March 2001.

OCCUPIED TERRITORY

THEY were all there: all that was left of them. Jesus was dead; dead and in his grave, and Judas lay in a shallow hole in the Potter's field, with a stake driven through his heart. They were all there: all that was left of them. Down the narrow street a dismal wind was blowing, spattering the rain against the streaming shutters, slatting drearily in the gusts.

Firelight glimmered dully on the smoky ceiling, making spectral shadows stir on the walls. The dishes on the dresser gleamed as the feeble flames flickered. Food and drink were set on the table; the cloth was wrinkled and soiled. They had not eaten; they had little stomach for food these days.

James and John were in the corner, their backs against the wall. John had been crying, but he was sleeping now, sobbing sometimes in his dream; his curly head resting on his brother's broad shoulder. James was not sleeping. His head was back, and his throat worked as he swallowed. His eyes were on the roof beams where they crossed.

Thomas had dragged a bench across the door, jamming it, and was huddled there, chin in the palm of his hand, his brown teeth gnawing at his nails.

At one end of the untidy table Andrew and Philip sat talking, their voices a deep rumbling whisper. Matthew was at the other end, staring into space. At his elbow was a frayed and rubbed leather purse, turned inside out, and in his fingers he was idly turning over a single copper coin.

Bartholomew was standing by the window, his back to the room, slouching, his shoulder against the jamb, seeing through the cracks in the banging shutter the windswept puddles and the slinking shadow of a prowling cat.

The other James, and Judas who insisted that he was Judas, but not Iscariot were asleep in the corner by the fire, their robes huddled about their heads, their feet stretched out to what little warmth there was.

And Peter sat before the fire, staring with sightless eyes into the embers: his face set and hard, his vague shadow glowering from the wall behind him.

Only the mutter of the two at the table, and the heavy breathing of the sleepers. Judas had a cold.

The candle on the wall was guttering and the fire was dying, and the wind was wailing.

There was a shuffle of sound far down the street. It grew louder and was the measured tramp of marching men. A hoarse challenge, the sound of a blow, a cry, a laugh. They knew what it was: the Roman watch on their rounds.

Bartholomew by the window straightened, holding his breath, his eyes glued to the crack, his left arm rigid behind him demanding silence.

Philip and Andrew stopped in the middle of a word: Thomas' fingers fumbled his wet lip. The sinews of James' arm bunched and hardened as it tightened about his brother's shoulders.

The sleepers by the fire were awake, tense on elbow and Judas' breath whistled in his nostrils. The knuckles of Peter's fist whitened as a man's knuckles do when his hand closes on the hilt of a sword. Then slackened.

Matthew's fingers fumbled, and the penny tinkled on to the floor, ran along the wood, and spun down, quicker and quicker, into silence.

The candle flickered once, twice, and went out, and a thin spiral of smoke rose from the red wick.

The stamp of masterful feet was growing nearer; a spear clanged on a shield. There was a mutter of voices, a curse, a snapped command.

The wind groaned in the chimney and bitter smoke belched into the room.

A mouse peeped out from the skirting, bright eyed, head cocked aside, savouring the silence.

The ring of marching feet passed on and up the street, and out of hearing. John sobbed in his throat. A coal fell from the fire. The shutter slammed against the sash. The scared mouse scuttered back to the skirting.

Thomas' bench went over with a crash. 'I can't stand it. I can't take it any more.'

The sweat was shining on his face. 'Last night they went by, and tonight they went by, and maybe tomorrow they'll go by. But they won't always go by. Why did he tell us to wait here? He's not coming back and we know he's not coming back. He'll never be back. He's dead: dead and buried. Deny it if you can. You saw it, John: you saw it, Peter, Andrew, Matthew. We all saw it. He's dead, I tell you. Let's get back to Galilee before these bloody Romans come pounding up the stair and break in that rickety door. And then, God help us, Pontius Pilate and eleven crosses on Golgotha.'

He was down on his knees, his hands across his face. No one spoke. There was no need to speak for there was nothing to say. It was plain as a pikestaff that Thomas was right.

Peter's lips were moving. Maybe he was praying, but by the look on his face, more likely he was cursing. Cursing himself, below his breath.

The face of James was hard and hopeless; only his hand was moving, soothing

John who was frightened. No one spoke. Why should they? There was nothing to say.

Andrew glanced at his brother, speculatively. He looked over to Philip, his eyes questioning: Philip shrugged his shoulders and looked away.

Bartholomew by the window took it all in: Thomas' outburst, the reaction of the rest of them to it. His eyes went round the dark room. He wiped the sweat from his face with the palm of his hand.

Quietly he moved over to the fire and threw on more kindling. He went over to the table and pulled the cloth straight. He poured what was left of the wine into the tankard, and cut bread. They followed him with their indifferent eyes.

He motioned Andrew, Philip and Matthew to rise, picked up the bench and set it straight; made as if to speak to Peter, and thought better of it; said to Andrew:

'Will you take the top of the table, Andy: you were the first of us.'

Andrew shook his head. 'I'm not a bit hungry, lad, but I suppose we'd better take a pick. God kens when we'll get another one.' He moved to the centre of the table and made to sit, looking across it at the fire. But Bartholomew stopped him with a gentle hand.

'No' there, Andy. That was his place yon night.' Andrew nodded and moved down a place. Philip sat beside him. Matthew stayed where he was. James pushed against the wall and rose to his feet.

'Come on Johnnie,' he said, stooping and taking John's hands in his own. 'You havena' eaten a thing all day', and pulled him to his feet.

Thomas looked up through his fingers, scrambled up and sat at the table sideways, looking at nobody. The two sleepers rubbed the sleep from their eyes and joined them.

Peter did not move, though he knew fine what was going on. He said nothing to them and they said nothing to him. They ate, crumbling the bread and dipping it in the wine as the tankard passed from hand to hand.

The room was very quiet. The empty space at the centre of the table loomed very large.

Bartholomew's lips were moving, he seemed to be speaking to himself. His eyes were far away. He was saying something in a low and reminiscent voice. They could hardly hear the whisper. Andrew stopped chewing his crust. James held the tankard halfway to his mouth. Thomas turned and listened. Peter raised his head. The voice went on. But was it Bartholomew's voice?

'This is my body which is broken for you; this do in remembrance of me. This cup is the new covenant in my blood which is shed for you. Ye are they which have continued with me in my temptations, and I appoint unto you a kingdom as my father hath appointed unto me, that ye may eat and drink at my table in my kingdom.'

The ten of them looked at Bartholomew with a strange surmise: the bread in his hands and a queer radiance on his kindly, ugly old face.

He broke the bread in his hand and gave to Philip and to Andrew, who in turn broke and passed it on: but Peter did not reach forward his hand. And as they ate, they heard what they heard and they saw what they saw.

Andrew felt the halt and stumble of a storm-tossed coble, and felt the sting of spindrift on his face. And there was one asleep between his knees who woke, and smiled, and said 'Peace be still.' And Andrew remembered how peaceful he had felt.

Matthew smelt the sourness of a crowd that thronged a hill, and heard a voice which said, 'Blessed are ye when men shall revile you for my sake.'

And Simon Zelotes heard the crash as the changers' tables went over, and saw above the press a long lithe arm that rose and fell, and heard the crack of a whip on beefy backs.

And John heard a well-loved voice that said, 'If ye love me, keep my commandments.'

And the brother of Jesus saw a joiner's yard, and a man who smoothed the oxen yokes and made them easy, with careful, understanding hands.

James saw a garden, and a pale face white under the moon, beaded with cold sweat, and a weary aching voice that said, 'Could ye not watch with me one hour?'

And Thomas saw the nailheads, and heard the thud of the hammer; and a thorn crowned ghastly face red streaked with blood; a face that still had the last of a smile when he said, 'Father, forgive them.'

Each had a vision, and a word, and a sign.

The sticks on the embers kindled, and suddenly the room was bright, and it seemed – could it be? – that there was the shape of a man in the empty chair; a shape that was not a shape, and yet it was: or was it just a trick of the firelight? But no, it was no trick of the firelight. And then the spell was broken.

'I saw him,' John laughed through the tears that were streaming down his cheeks. 'I saw him. He said, "Love me as I loved you".'

'It was "peace, be still", I heard.' And Andrew laughed too.

'Could ye not watch with me one hour?' That was what James said, and in a tone that promised he would not fail again.

'He said, "Behold my hands and feet",' said Thomas, very quietly. "And I saw his hands, the sore, sore hands of him.'

'He was raging through the temple.' This was Zelotes.

'He was back on the hill,' that was Matthew.

'I feel a new man now. I'm ready for anything: everything,' that was all of them.

'What about you, Peter,' said Bartholomew, in an uncertain kind of a voice. 'What did you hear?'

'I heard a cock crow.'

They looked blankly, the one at the other.

'I dare not eat this bread. I dare not drink this wine.' Peter's face was terrible. 'I denied him. Satan he called me once. Get thee behind me, Satan, he said. And he was right. He was always right, for Satan I am, bedevilled and damned. Judas is dead; aye, he's dead. He went out into the dark and he hanged himself. And that's what I should have done. I should have cut my own damned throat. And I would have too, but my hand would not hold the knife. I'll go out now. It's dark enough for a hanging.'

'Do you hear the wind? That's no wind. That's the fiends of the pit calling; and they're calling me. Not you: just me, Simon Peter, the traitor. Simon Peter the big shot. Simon Peter who denied him. I should go out to them the way Judas did. I should go out and hang myself the way Judas did. But I can't. I'm scared. I'm scared to live and I'm scared to die.'

James raised his hand as if to clap Peter on the back, as a friend would to a friend in trouble. But thought better of it, and let his hand fall to his side.

'But, Peter,' he said, 'We all failed him, Peter. We all did in our own way. But you see what's happened to us here tonight. You see the difference it's made. I . . . we . . . we don't feel bad about it any more. We see now that he always wanted to die, and to die yon way. But he doesn't want us to die: not yet anyway. There's something we've got to do before we die. I know it, Peter. He's depending on us. There is nobody else. That's why he told us to stay together and remember him.'

'Take the bread, Peter; take the cup and drink as we did yon night. It's not Bartholomew who's giving it to you. It's himself. Peter, take it old friend, for auld lang syne's sake.'

Red in the fireglow, Peter's face was tortured: the face of a man who could smell the red hot hobs of hell.

'For auld lang syne, says you? We all failed him, quo' he? But I saw his face when they took him away. I saw his face in the High Priest's court, and you didn't: none of you heard the cock crow. But I did.'

There was nothing they could say. They had all failed, but this man Peter had failed most terribly. And they knew it; and he knew it; and he knew that they knew it.

The room was very dark now: only a dim glow on the ring of gaunt strained faces.

'Thou art Peter'. A voice, and Peter knew that voice, and only Peter heard it, but they all knew he was hearing something: and they all knew what that something was. Andrew looked over to Bartholomew, and he nodded and fixed his eyes again on Peter's face.

'Thou art Peter, and upon this rock will I build my church, and the gates of hell shall not prevail against it.'

Peter reached out his hand and took the bread. He was on his knees now: they were all on their knees. Peter took the bread and broke and ate, and his mouth was dry and he found it hard to swallow. A crumb fell from his shaking hand. He took the wine cup and as his fingers shook, the good wine slopped over the brim.

The wind was rising again, howling like the legions of the lost across the slatting shutter.

'Peace I leave with you; my peace give I unto you. Not as the world gives I give unto you. Let not your heart be troubled, neither let it be afraid.'

They looked at one another, their eyes wide with a great amazement, and the voice went on, thrilling the darkening room.

'All power is given unto me in heaven and earth; go ye therefore, and teach all nations, baptising them in the name of the father and of the son and of the Holy Ghost. Teaching them to observe all things whatsoever I have commanded you; and lo, I am with you always, even unto the end of the world.'

For a little longer they stayed on their knees, waiting. But the voice did not speak again.

Far down the street came the sound of marching men. They were silent, wondering, waiting for someone to make the first move. Bartholomew was looking at Thomas, with quizzical, curious eyes. And Thomas grinned over to Batholomew, grinned, and laughed aloud, and sprang to his feet, and pounded on the table.

'Let us praise God,' he shouted, and began to sing:
'God is your refuge and strength, a very present help in trouble;
Therefore we will not fear though the earth be removed,
And though the mountains be carried into the midst of the sea.'
The others were joining in, their backs were straight, their heads were high.
'The Lord of Hosts is with us The God of Jacob is our refuge.'
Spears were rattling below in the street.
'He maketh wars to cease unto the ends of the earth,
He breaketh the bow and cutteth the spear in sunder.
He burneth the chariot in the fire.

Be still, and know that I am God
I will be exalted among the heathen,
I will be exalted in the earth.
The Lord of Hosts is with us,
The God of Jacob is our refuge.'

The watch passed down the street, laughing at the singing and wondering what it was all about. There was no accounting for these Jews around Passover time. Or at any other time for that matter.

The last Amen trailed into silence. Peter was the leader again.

'Come, you fishers of men,' he roared. 'The world is wide, and it's all outside. Who's for a road with a cross at the end of it, and be damned to them?'

'We're all with you, Simon.'

'Lead on Peter.'

'Your road's our road, you old reprobate.'

There was a scrambling into heavy clothes; a tightening of sandal thongs. Judas opened the door with a footman's flourish, and two by two, offering an arm politely as if they were going to a ball, they went out, and down the stair, and into the night and the wind and the rain.

And the spirit they left behind them was content to see them go, and the light of that spirit was about them as they went. And the room was quiet again; the rumpled cloth, the dishes, the bread, the bashed tankard. And a coal caught and flickered.

Down the narrow street the wind still mourned, and the shutter banged in the gusts; and up from the street to the silent room came laughter and the sound of splashing footsteps, that passed on and up and out of hearing.

The mouse peeped out from the skirting, tasting the welcome strange silence; pattered into the room like a shadow: over to the fireplace like a blown leaf.

There was a crumb of bread, and the mouse nibbled at it. There was a bright penny; and a puddle of wine that in the fireglow grew rich, for a moment, like a man's blood.

EASTER IS ALWAYS

WHAT THE UNDERTAKER SAID

THE undertaker and I were last out of the house; the male mourners were well on their way down the tenement stairs. And they had made the most of their mourning. You could still hear the wailings of the women, although the door was shut.

Standing on the landing, the undertaker ran the cuff of his right sleeve round his hat, clapped it on his head, and settled it with a firm tap.

'It's well seen,' said he, 'that they're not members of the kirk.'

Of course he and I are together a lot at the funerals of folk who are not members of mine or of any other church, and I thought this might just be an intelligent guess on his part. I said, 'How do you make that out, Bob?'

As we went downstairs he told me. 'I can always tell,' said he. 'You don't get all this weeping and wailing with church folk – and I don't care what church they are. You just don't get it.'

'Bob,' said I, 'you're right, though I never thought of it like that. It does make a difference, and a mighty big one at that.'

So down to the waiting cars we went, and to the waiting cemetery. The cemetery of Greenook is on a hill, well wooded, and on a summer's day when you stand at the graveside, there are larks in the lift above you, and thrush and blackbird are busy in the bushes. Before you and below, there is the lovely sweep of the Firth of Clyde from Dumbarton Rock to the hills of Arran. The mountains of Cowal lie out to the north, and beyond them the Grampians shoulder for room. But in winter, when the south west wind is whipping in from the Atlantic swaying the funereal trees, and the rain drips from the umbrellas, and the cold clay is cold indeed; then even the stoutest heart can shrink as the dust goes back to dust. It was such a day, the day I am speaking of.

'I am the resurrection and the life, sayeth the Lord. He that believeth in me shall never die. Let not your hearts be troubled; in my father's house are many mansions.' The same words when the sun is bright and the larks are singing; the same words when the rain drips from cypress and laurel, and shines on the spades and the wet clay by the graveside.

I spoke the great words of scripture and then the committal. The coffin was lowered by the eight nearest of kin as our Scottish custom is, and we turned away. And I wondered what it all meant to them.

It's hardly a question you can ask at such a time, and so I still do not know. I don't suppose that even good Christians could quite answer the question to express the deep down feeling that the old mission hymn calls *Blessed Assurance*.

It's something you either have or you don't have. You feel the pangs of grief just as grievously as any other does, and maybe more so, for in every way you are a better person and more genuine. You do not know how the dead rise, or when the dead rise. In fact you do not very much care, for you know that they do rise, and you know why they rise.

You know that in the end of the day the last word is not with the clay and the spade and the worm. You know that the last word is with the lark and the blackbird and with the risen Lord.

So you stand in the rain by an open grave, surrounded by all the signs of man's mortality; but you know that you are immortal, and so you fling into the teeth of death the defiance of the Christian: "O death where is thy sting? O grave where is thy victory?"

Yes, Easter is always: not just on the Sunday that celebrates our Saviour's rising, but always. For man lives in an Easter world, though not all men and women live as if it was that kind of world. In one way the last word is never with the undertaker, but in another way it was that day, when he said, 'Mr Dow, you can always tell.'

WHAT THE ENGINEER SAID

THE fitting shop was a thunder of sound for there was a new ship's engine on test. The engineer was standing by and I said to him, 'How's she going, Mac?'

'Fine, man; fine,' said he, 'all things considered.' And I asked him what he meant by 'all things considered.' He wiped his hands on a sweat rag and made a minute adjustment to a valve.

'Well you see, he went on, 'she's got to shake down yet. She's juist a lot o' pairts the noo, and there's still a wee roughness till they begin to work thigither. But she's not at all bad, and that's what I mean by all things considered.' I nodded that I understood, and he went on.

'Now that I've given you an answer to your complete satisfaction, I wonder if ye'll be guid enough tae dae the same for me?' I said I'd be delighted if I could, and asked him what the question was.

'It's about what you were saying the ither day,' said he. 'You were talking about the kirk-goin' man and woman keeping their tears tae themsel's. And I said tae mysel' when I heard ye; says I, that's a' verra weel, and I could agree wi' ye gin the one that's gaen is ane that has been wearyin' lang syne for their lang hame, and gaes til it in the natural wey o' things. There's nae cause for mournin' there, surely. Fowk get wore out the same wey that this engine'll get wore out, and there's naething tae break your heart about in that. But that's nae the wey folk aye gae. Whiles it's a pititu' business a'thegither. A young ane wi' his hale life afore him that's nippit aff; or a man that dwines awa' and leaves a widow and a hantle o' bairns; or a little ane knocked down wi' a bus, or taen awa' wi' polio. It's nae juist sae easy tae say 'Thy will be done' when your heart's near breakin' in your briest.'

I reminded him that I had not said that it is ever easy to part with someone you love.

'Fair enough,' said he, 'I'll grant ye that, but what wey does it have tae happen ava? What wey does God nae get rid o' a' the ill things that hurt and hinder?'

'Like you with the engine?' I asked.

'Exactly,' said he. 'I ken a' that's gaen intil this engine here: the plans and the plane table, the lining up, the turning, moulding, casting, welding, finishing, fitting, and a' the rest o't. Efter the job's done we try it out. If we think there's one bit that's no' a' it should be, then out wi't and in wi' anither. This job's got tae be dependable – as dependable as Clydebuilt can mak' her. Now if human beings like me can dae that wi' cauld iron and steel, what's tae hinder God daen the same wi' the raw material o' his ain creation? What's tae hinder him daen it wi' us, that the guid buik says are made in his verra image? What wey canna we gae turning awa' sweetly till auld age and weariness comes owre us in the course o' time and we're rung til a stop – feenished wi' engines? Can ye answer me that?'

'I'll try,' said I, and I asked him a question.

'Isn't it true, Mac, that's there's a lot of things can happen to that engine of yours that will be due to the way the engine's run, not to any fault in the way the engine was made?'

He said that was true: that there were as many fools below deck as above.

'And it's true too,' I went on, 'that this engine's designed to do a special job. If you try to do anything else with it, it won't work.' He nodded. I went on, 'And I think,' said I, 'that when this engine's fitted there will be instructions with it, and a strong recommendation about the quality of the fuel?' Again he nodded. 'Then,' said I, 'isn't it a wee bit unfair to blame God the Maker for all the faults of the running and the fuel and the engineer?'

He agreed with that, and he could hardly do otherwise. Then I said, 'You won't deny that our Lord's life was the most wonderful of all – because he followed the design of the Maker.'

'I'll grant ye that,' said he, 'but the Lord was different. There's what ye were speaking about yesterday – Easter is always. I'm sure naebody's dune what he did, naebody afore or since.'

'I wouldn't be so sure of that,' said I. 'All graves are empty.'

'Natural causes,' said he.

I said, 'Of course, Mac. What other causes are there?' I went on, 'When you're driven by the power that drove the Lord Jesus, who are we to say what's natural and what's not natural? First there was sail, then steam, triple expansion, turbine, diesel, gas turbine, and now zeta; power, power and more power.'

'True enough for the engine, he interrupted, as he threw the wheel and the breathing, pulsing, thundering engine stopped at the end of its twenty four hours of running, and his voice became loud in the sudden silence. True enough for the engine, but how div ye get the power for yourself?'

'You ask for it, Mac,' I said. 'You ask for it.'

WHAT THE POLITICIAN SAID

IT was shortly after the Glasgow rectorial egg and flour battle that I ran across the politician, and he was still bristling with indignation. I agreed with him when he said it was a disgraceful business.

'I don't mind interruptions,' said he, hastening to show me how broad minded he was, 'I don't mind those, we get plenty of them in our line of business from time to time, but flour bombs and rotten eggs is just going beyond the limit.

'It is indeed,' said I, 'except for one thing: that flour bombs could so easily be real bombs.'

'Surely not in Britain,' he protested, 'come, come, now.'

He was quite amused at the idea. Like so many other people he had not realised that the people who throw real bombs are just the people who have never been allowed to throw flour bombs. Politicians sometimes forget that a well directed egg is a democratic gesture in its own right.

Not that I make any excuse for hooliganism, but it is never a bad thing to let politicians know that they rule by the tolerant permission of a free people. My politician asked me if I thought they did forget that.

'Yes,' said I, 'sometimes you do. Sometimes you forget that something happened in a garden at Jerusalem long ago, which has made all the difference in the world to the rights of human beings.'

'You mean Easter?' he asked.

'Yes,' said I, 'I mean Easter. All of a sudden life became different. All of a sudden folk realised that they were immortal. And the moment they discovered that, was the moment when they began to say to themselves and to their rulers: 'It is one thing for mortals to bow their knee to the tyrant and their neck to the yoke; but we are not mortals. We are immortals.'

'Of course death does make us all equal,' said the politician, rather piously.

'No,' said I, 'it does nothing of the sort. It is not mortality that makes us equal it is immortality. We are all equals not because we die, but because we don't die. Because we live in an Easter world. Because in the sight of God we are all precious enough to be preserved forever. That is what makes us equal, and by the same token, that is what makes us free.'

'But you must have authority,' said the politician. 'You must have law, you must have regulations. Society would be a shambles without them.'

'I'm afraid society is rather a shambles with them,' said I. 'What a change it would be, though, to see rules and regulations for immortals rather than laws and controls for mere mortals. For so many of your rules deal with the things that Jesus said were of no importance whatever; they deal with the things you leave behind you when you die; not with the things you take with you. Every time the church or the parson opens his mouth on matters of politics there's an outcry for them to mind their own business. But everyone seems to forget that religion is the only authority whose laws of behaviour and rules of conduct take any account of the fact that you are not finished when you die.'

'What else can we do?' he protested. 'We're dealing with people, and human nature being what it is . . .'

'But here I had to interrupt him for he was so terribly wrong. Human nature is not what people are showing these days: that's inhuman nature. Human nature is that wonderful, precious, undying quality which makes us the children of God; which the Lord Jesus died to proclaim; which he proved to be human nature because he proved it to be God's nature. We are trying to live as if Easter had never been; we are trying to live as if life begins in a National Health Service maternity ward and ends in a municipal cemetery. We are wrong, for that is not life. Life comes from God and to God it returns. Easter has been, and Easter is always.

WHAT THE HOUSEWIFE SAID

THE housewife poured out a cup of tea, inquired about the sugar and milk, and asked me if I would like a wee scone. I don't know why all scones are referred to as 'wee' and folk never seem to have big ones. But I took the wee scone, and after some remarks about the state of the weather and the health of some mutual friends the talk turned to more serious matters, and I told her what the undertaker and the engineer and the politician had said to me. She agreed very much with the undertaker.

'There'a many a time,' she said, 'when I've been real ashamed of some of my friends, and other times when I've been that proud of them I had to tell them. Of course it's true that your faith makes the difference when death comes knocking on the door. It's all saved up and stored away inside you. The lessons you learned in Sunday school, the hymns you've sung and the prayers you've prayed; the bits you remember from the Bible; the sermons that touched you. You could never put it in words, but it's there all the time. And so when the bad day comes, everything comes running to your help.'

'It's like my mother when she used to set a good bowl of broth down in front of us, made with a good nap bone, and we would say that the wee lassie across the landing was getting sausage to her dinner. My mother used to say her broth will stand by you better than all the sausages that were ever fried.'

'And so they did, for when the measles and the whooping cough broke out in the school, maybe we'd get them like the rest, but we got over them quicker. All the good substance we'd taken day in day out came to help us. That's what I always tell mine. Put what's good and wholesome into your stomach and into your head, and it'll stand by you when you need it. I've never known it to fail.'

'And what about the engineer?' I asked her. She smiled.

'Him?' she said. 'Just like a man. They will have it that folk are like engines, and here they're not like that at all. They aye want to know the why and the where and the wherefore: all drawn on a board and set down on paper. And religion's not like that at all.

'There's my own Jock, and a better man never came home on a Friday with his pay-poke the way he got it. Jock doesna trouble the kirk very muckle, and when you ask him why, what does he say?'

'He begins by saying he takes a wee dram now and again, and he thinks the kirk disapproves of that. And he's too shy to sing the hymns in case somebody hears him. And when he does hear a sermon he wants to ken what that has to do with the shipyards. And then he runs into somebody he doesna like, and minds that one's a pillar of the kirk, and he begins to talk about hypocrites and all that. Then he gets warmed up and wants to ken what Nehemiah has to do with Nasser, or Caiaphas with Khrushchev. He says he doesna want to hear what Paul said to the Ephesians and all that sort of thing.'

'Perfectly legitimate objections', I said.

'Oh aye,' said the housewite, 'of course they are. But where he's all mixed up is thinking that's religion. All the time, away deep down inside himself, the real thing's there. He's just naturally a good man if he'd only admit it to himself. I whiles think that our bit house here is not unlike the house at Bethany, you know.'

'And which are you,' I asked, 'Mary or Martha.' She smiled.

'Whiles the one,' she said, 'And whiles the other. But there's one thing I'm sure of: Jack is Lazarus, for I always think of Lazarus sitting quiet in his corner when he came home from his work, smoking his pipe and just listening when Jesus came to bide with them. Just a man like Jock. And I ken the Lord will do for Jack what he did for Lazarus lang syne.'

And I thought how right she was, for Jesus gave Lazurus the victory over the grave, because he loved his friend and the folk of Bethany.

All families are eternal; Easter tells you that. A family never dies, but is always passing from one generation to another the likeness, the tradition, the very nature. But more than that, Easter means, far more than that. It means that somewhere and somehow the family lives forever. For Easter is always.

WHAT THE DOCTOR SAID

MY friend the doctor is not what Scots folk used to call 'Kirk greedy.' But that is not because he is either atheist or agnostic. It isn't because in his student days when he was doing anatomy, he couldn't find any cavity in a human body which could house a human soul. It's not cynical or scientific knowledge which keeps him away. It's just that he has always been pretty busy and pretty tired, and constantly at the beck and call of a lot of folk who hadn't much the matter with them, but who might have had for all he knew when they telephoned him.

He got out of the way of going, that's all. So that when he talks about religion he's usually a bit shy, and not at all hard and worldly. Of course folk don't say 'worldly' nowadays. They call it 'being practical and facing the facts.'

Anyone who has as much to do as a doctor has with people in the extremities of their lives, either gets a sour outlook on humanity, or he gets a tremendous respect and admiration for human beings. My friend's point of view is sometimes the one and sometimes the other. It was on the evening of Easter Sunday that I had my last crack with him.

After he had asked me how the Easter services had gone, and I had told him, I asked him what he had been doing all day. It turned out that it had been an ordinary day. There had been a birth, there had been a death, and in between these two there had been the usual run of illnesses serious and slight. He used the word 'ordinary' two or three times as he described his day, and I asked him if he was doing it deliberately.

He smiled and said he was glad I had noticed it. Yes, he had meant it deliberately. And I asked him why.

'It's like this,' said he. 'You can't ever help to bring a baby into the world without thinking about Christmas; and you can't ever watch anyone die without thinking about Easter. You can divide folk pretty well into two classes: those who think about Christmas and Easter at times like that, and those who don't.'

He went on: 'I'm concerned in these events so much and so often that Christmas becomes any day, and Easter becomes any day. I don't know what doctors in Judea long ago used to think, but sometimes I wonder if the child they were helping into the world might be the Messiah that the people were praying for.'

I always wonder, at a birth, what that child will be like when its time comes to die.

'And I never see anybody die, but I wonder how they are managing with the stone that was rolled across the tomb. I always wonder how they are getting on as they go through the Easter mystery.'

Almost to myself I said, 'Easter is always.' He heard me.

'That's it exactly,' said he. 'Easter is always. Every day hundreds of people in this land are in the middle of their own Easter. They're going through this strange experience of going to sleep in one world and waking up in another. And that's why I say you can divide people into two classes: those who believe that it is an experience their dead pass through, and those who don't.'

'Religion to me,' the doctor went on, 'is not a case of remembering Christmas once a year and Easter once a year and living a reasonably respectable life in general. To me it means that when a child is born you know that the real new life is not new at all. It has come from the mystery that is God. It means that when you stand in the presence of death, you know that the real life has not ended; the real life of the person lying there no longer a person, has gone back to God. For me, every day is Christmas, and Easter is always.

THE LISTENER. WHAT DO YOU SAY?

THE first time I preached in a broadcast service from my church in Greenock, I thought long and hard about the congregation. Not the congregation in the pews taking active part in the service, but the congregation of listeners: listeners like yourself at this moment.

What kind of people were you? How were you listening? What were you needing from me? Could I give you what you were needing?

After all the thought, it came to me that the listeners would be almost exactly the same kind of folk as the hearers in the church. In these broadcasts there has been no hearer in the studio, there has just been you and me.

Who are you, my friend, and what have you been hoping to hear, and have you heard it? Or has your listening been casual? Are you really waiting for the time signal and the news, rather than for a religious message from me – the good news?

But whoever you are, has anything come to you from God, by way of me? Anything about Easter? Anything to send you out to live more confidently? I do not know: I can only hope and pray that it may be so. If by chance or by intention you have heard all of these talks, I hope that you will believe me when I say that these characaters with whom I have had conversation in your hearing, were not imaginary, but real. They are composite, of course; a mixture each of many. But they are real. People like these have said things like that to me many a time. What I am wondering now is if you, as a person, have recognised your own particular point of view: have in a way seen yoursel as the undertaker, the engineer, the politician, the housewife, the doctor. Or whether there is some other point of view which I have not expressed at all.

Mind you I don't profess to be able even to begin to explain Easter, and it's a very silly man who would try to do it in five, five-minute talks. But they do not call this morning five minutes, 'Educate your minds', they call it 'Lift up your hearts.' I can only hope and trust that some at least of you have gone out to the day with your hearts lifted a little. For Easter is not a new way of dying; it is a new way of living. Life, not death is its message. None of us know just when or where we will die. To believe that Easter is always, should make us not at all afraid of it where and when it comes. But that is not by any means the whole message of Easter. Be your life short or long, be it still near its beginning, or be it not far from its end, Easter for you means that you are a very extraordinary person. You are, in fact, a person who does not die at all. You are an immortal. If it was suddenly revealed to you that everyone in the world was mortal except yourself, you would think you were the luckiest person alive; and so, maybe, you would be. All the religions of the world are full of the story of men and women who spent their lives seeking the secret of eternal life. If they thought they had discovered it, and managed to persuade other folk that they had discovered it, they were worshipped as if they were gods. For they had found the most wonderful of all knowledge.

Maybe it is because we have a vague idea that everyone is immortal that we don't excite ourselves more over the fact that we personally are immortal. But it is an exciting thought.

Say to yourself, 'I, myself, me; this person of my name, sitting at this address, listening to this talk, will never die. I am an immortal.'

There's something worth making a song about. Make it a song, then. Go out and sing it; sing it by living like a person who cannot die. Lift up your hearts. Easter is always.

THE MORNING AFTER THE NIGHT BEFORE

THE Prodigal Son opened his eyes and wondered where on earth he was. He was in bed. But where?

He pushed back the blankets and sat up with a jerk. Which was unwise, for his head felt as if there was a small cannon ball rumbling about under the skull. He closed his eyes till it settled down again, and then gingerly opened them.

Now he knew what bed it was. It was his own. He was back in the old bed in the old room in the old house. And it hadn't changed a bit.

Years ago he had screwed two knobs off the bedposts and lost them. They were still lost. There was the same patchwork quilt, the same faded but still impossibly blue roses forming fours on the cam-ceiled walls. The same mirror advertising sheep dip hung above the washstand, the same framed text above the iron fireplace: *'What doth the Lord require of thee but to do justly and to love mercy, and to walk humbly with thy God.'*

He looked at it for a long minute. He might have got away with the first two requirements, but not with the third. He hadn't walked very humbly with anyone: till he got tired of the pigs.

Very circumspectly he swung his legs over the side of the bed and put his feet on the cold waxcloth. The only shoes were the good ones that were always kept for the honoured guest when he had taken his wellingtons off. He slipped his feet into them, stood up, and went slowly over to the washstand.

The same cracked ewer and basin, and what looked suspiciously like the same cake of carbolic soap. The water was cold. He appreciated it.

He opened the press where he used to hang his clothes when he remembered. It was empty. Of course he had been wearing his good suit when he went away. He'd given the others to Tammie Glen the orraman. There was just his brother's Sunday suit hanging on the back of the chair. No wonder brother had been annoyed last night. He dressed and came downstairs.

The farmhouse was going like a mill. No wonder, the work was all behind. They'd all slept in, and some of them looked as if they'd have been better to stay in bed. There would be a bit of tidying up to do, too. He thought he'd be better out of the road. He opened the parlour door and went in.

They don't have parlours nowadays, but his mother and father were old fashioned people; their good room was still the parlour.

The horsehair chairs that were so jaggy on the backs of your bare knees on a

Sunday. Sunday was the only day you got into the parlour unless there were special visitors. The stiff armchairs that Queen Victoria would have approved of with the antimacassars on their backs. The walnut piano with the fretwork front and the modesty vest of red silk. The plush tablecover with the pom-poms, and the overmantel with china ornaments brought back from the holidays, each with the crest of the holiday town. Not that there had been many holidays. The marble timepiece like a tombstone, the hairy rug, the aspidistra in a green pot, the picture of the highland cattle standing in a loch in front of a sunset like a fried egg.

They haven't been long getting it back to normal, the Prodigal thought to himself as he stood in the doorway looking round the grey room. It had been different last night. Last night all the furniture had been shoved to the sides and they'd had the carpet up in seconds, and in no time there were as many glasses on the piano as there were sound keys in it. And over by the window, Tammie Glen with his fiddle, and when Tammie played the Reel o' Tulloch he could even make the the foot of a bed tap time. Aye, Tammie had worked for his dram last night. But now it was morning, and a gey cheerless morning it was, too.

He moved over to the small window and looked out. The rain was dripping from the slates, and there wasn't a living thing in sight but a bedraggled hen on the axle of an upturned cart.

Then Tammie Glen crossed the yard wheeling a barrow of dung, and with every jolt of the wheel on the cobbles he screwed up his face like a man in pain.

And yonder was the road winding up and over the hill. The road that once had been the rainbow road with the crock of gold at its foot. The road he had taken with a swing in his stride and a lilt in his heart. The road he had dragged himself over yesterday with all pride gone, thinking, who will answer the door? What will they say when they see me?

And then his father blind with tears, and all of them with their arms round him, and in half an hour the parlour like the Jolly Beggars. And there it was now, as thoroughly respectable as Presbyterianism.

Last night and this morning. And after today was tomorrow, and tomorrow was the Sabbath. The cracked bell would ding its summons, and from the farms and crofts around the folk would come out in their twos, with the bairns in procession behind. The wifies in their braws and the men in their blue suits with their boots shining and the tags sticking up at the back. And the lads and lassies! The lads he'd laughed at the night before he went away adventuring, and the lassies that could not sleep o' nights wearying for him.

Aye, there would be a big turn out on the Sabbath, now that they knew he was back. He was willing to bet they would start with Coleshill: *'Who thy diseases all and pains doth heal, and thee forgive.'*

What did they know of infirmities? Or the pain of being forgiven? Even now he could feel his ears burning. They were talking about him. He was today's only subject for conversation.

And after Sunday there was Monday and Tuesday and the procession of the days and weeks and months and years trudging on to the end of time. And over in the bothie Tammie Glen had decided it was too wet for work, and his head must have been better since he got his dinner, and he had his fiddle tuned, and the sound of it went through the Prodigal like a knife. He swore beneath his breath, but not quite as much beneath his breath as he had meant. For a voice spoke to him.

'D'ye ken what's for the dinner the day, Jock?' He had not seen his grannie in the big chair with its back to the door, facing the cold grate with the coloured tissue paper in it.

'No, grannie,' he said without turning. 'And I can't say I'm caring very much.'

'It's cold veal,' she said in a voice as cold as the veal. 'We didnae finish it last night.'

And he began to laugh, but it was a laugh with no fun in it, as a laugh should have. Cold veal for the dinner fairly put the lid on it. His grannie waited till he was done.

'Aye, it's gey fushionless farin', Jock. I'm no' a' that keen on it mysel'.' And she laughed and there was fun in the laugh.

'Then that's the two of us, grannie'. This time his laugh was better. The old lady chuckled awhile, as if over a recollection

'Aweel, Jock,' she said, 'ye'd better make the best o't, for it's the last ye'll see o' the fancy things for a whiley, I doubt. It's auld clae's and parritch for you frae now on. So ye'd better get tae like it, and a' that gaes wi' it. Dae ye think ye can manage?'

'I don't know, grannie.' He was still looking out at the rain. 'I just don't know.'

'I dinna see what way not.' Her voice had taken on rather an edge. 'I can put up wi't.'

'I've no doubt you can, grannie,' he said in a kindly tone, and turning towards her, though she was still hidden behind the high back of the chair. 'But you're different.'

He started to walk up and down before the window, like a dog on a chain.

'You're used to it, grannie. You've never known anything else. And, let's face it, grannie, you're not just as young as you used to be. That fiddle of Tammie Glen's . . . it's just a fiddle to you; but for me it could be the pipes of Pan.'

26

He stopped and faced the window again. Tammie was in full spate.

His grannie sniffed. It wasn't as if she had a cold in her head. It was the other kind of sniff. And when she spoke, her voice was sharper still.

'And where did you get the notion, Jock, that you're the only one that's ever been to the far country?'

'I've no such notion, grannie,' he said quietly. 'I met a few others when I was there.'

'Then what gave you the notion that you're the first or the last that ever came back from it?' She paused for a moment, then added, as a sort of throw away line. 'What about me?'

That shook him. 'You grannie!' he said with at least a couple of exclamation marks after it. He swung round on his heel, his mouth wide open in amazement.

'Aye me.' 'And was there a trace of an old satisfaction in her voice? He crossed over slowly, and went down on one knee at the side of her chair.

'Tell me about it grannie. Just between you and me, and I'll never breathe a word. Where did you go? What ploys did you get up to?'

'I'll no' tell ye that, Jock.' She smiled and rumpled his hair. 'In the first place, it's none of your business, and in the second, there's little difference atween one far country and anither. And the daft things this ane does or that ane does when they get there.'

'Then tell me how you came home, grannie.' He laid his hand on her's where it rested on the arm of the chair. She laid her other hand on his, and squeezed it.

'Just by the same road as yoursel', Jock. And wi' the same thought: make me a servant, for I'm fit for nothing better.'

'And then, grannie?' he whispered, knowing the answer all the time. She laughed and then she sighed.

'New clae's and a bonnie gowden ring. New shoes on my tired feet, an' the fatted calf for our supper . . .'

'And the next day . . . cold veal for your dinner?' He laughed, a real laugh this time.

'Aye, Jock, the very same. Cold veal for a start, and then auld clae's and parritch. And I've been taking them and the likes o' them ever since.

'And liking it, grannie ?' His eyes were smiling. So were hers. 'Not all the time Jock, to be honest wi' ye. But taking them just the same . . .'

He rose and stood behind her chair, his hands on her shoulders.

'Was nothing changed, grannie, when you came home? Was it all just the same . . . like this?'

'Just the same, Jock.' She rose, leaning on her stick which was standing against the arm of the chair. 'Nothing changed at all, but me.' She began to walk stiffly towards the door, and went through when he opened it for her, leaving him with his thoughts that were not very happy thoughts.

For it is not easy to face the fact that when you come back to God, or even when you come to God for the very first time in the excitement of a conversion, it doesn't go on at this high and exciting level. That you've just to carry on where you left off, and that's all about it. The party doesn't last forever. All that you left half done is still there, half done, waiting for you to finish it.

O yes, it's a great life, the home-coming; it's a great excitement, the conversion. They're all so glad to see you. For a while. But not for long; not for very long.

And then all that's for it is to buckle to and try to make a go of it; or head for the far country again and try to make another go of it: this time with better hopes than the pigs' brock. After all, you know things now that you didn't know before.

He was still thinking this way when the door half opened and his grannie looked round the edge of it.

'Your dinner's on the table, Jock. Will I tell them you're just coming?'

And he laughed and stepped over, and offered his arm like a lord to a lady.

'Yes, grannie, I'll take my dinner and try to like it. But O grannie I wish Tammie Glen would give over that damn fiddle.'

THE DOOR

THEY sat together by the fire, for it had grown chilly in the forecourt of heaven: four men. One large and broad and generously bearded with a face harsh and strong; one small and slight, his lank black hair plastered to one side over his brow, a small dark moustache, a face deeply lined and with fanatic eyes; the third was a small man too; but a small grey man; straggly grey hair, straggly grey beard, and an exceedingly bright eye in his head; the fourth was a great chunky, solid man with hair brushed straight back, and a heavy black moustache that hid the full mouth.

The ancients used to divide the nature of man into four classes, named after the elements of earth, air, fire, and water. These were men of fire: hot men, impatient men.

Stalin was speaking when I came closer to hear what the great ones had to say.

'Looking from here and seeing it all whole for the first time, I've got to admit that the world below is in quite a mess. What do you think, Paul?'

Paul smiled a little ruefully. 'Sometimes I prefer not to think too much about it, Joseph. But if you look closely you can see that there's still a deal of good in struggling man too. This was bound to happen, of course.'

'Yes,' said Moses, 'It was bound to happen. You can't keep breaking the law and expect to get away with it all the time.'

'Your law, of course,' Hitler sneered. 'Not a bad law, of course, as long as you're a Jew.'

'Thank you, Adolph.' Moses winked at Paul, and Stalin smiled and lit his pipe. 'We are quite a people, we Jews, you know,' Moses went on. 'We were a civilised people when your Nordic ancestors were gnawing buffalo bones in the bogs of Rhineland, and knocking lumps off one another with stone clubs.'

'I'd be very happy to know what our friend admires in us most,' said Paul looking as if he was desperately anxious to know, which he wasn't.

'Not in all of you,' Hitler growled. He had no sense of humour at all. 'But I have a reluctant admiration for Moses: not for you, Paul. But for Moses. He was a man of action, he achieved his ambition.'

Moses slowly shook his head. 'Alas, no, my friend. You have not read the book aright. I did not set foot in the Promised Land. I had no more than a sight of it from the top of Mount Pisgah.'

Stalin took the pipe from his mouth. 'We all had our Pisgah,' he grunted. 'No man ever gets further than Pisgah. It's those who come after him who cross Jordan and enter the inheritance.'

'Yes,' Paul nodded. 'That is very true. But the great thing about reaching your Pisgah is that there for the first time you realise that it wasn't just a dream, and that there really is a Promised Land.'

'I agree with you up to a point,' said Moses. 'If you are to die with no more than the vision of the dream, you can go fairly happily as long as you know there's a good man ready to take over from you. A man like Joshua.'

'A man like Timothy,' said Paul.

Hitler and Stalin sat brooding, and saying nothing. Maybe Stalin was thinking of Krushchev. If he was he didn't look very enthusiastic. Finally Hitler whispered, 'I had nobody.'

The silence was growing a wee bit uncomfortable when Paul cleared his throat and said quietly, and looking at no one in particular, 'What kind of story are you going to tell when you go through the door?'

That shook them. Stalin and Hitler looked round apprehensively.

Hitler said, swallowing the lump in his throat, 'What door?'

Stalin pointed with his pipe: 'You don't mean that door?'

'The very same,' said Moses.

'But that's not a door, that's a fixture.' Stalin felt for his matches. 'Look, there's no handle on it.'

'The handle,' said Paul gently, 'is on the other side. It opens only from the other side, when they're ready for you.'

'I can wait.' Stalin wasn't easily put out. 'And anyway I don't have to make excuses for anything I did.'

'Don't you?' Paul's eyebrows went up. 'You are very lucky; very lucky indeed.'

'If they want to know anything about me, they'll get it in the book.'

'Same with me, Stalin,' Hitler nodded with more assurance than he felt. 'Same with me, it's all in my book.'

'I can say the same, you know,' Moses smiled. 'So can Paul.' And Paul nodded.

'All in the book,' he agreed. 'The trouble is that you can't just be sure that they've read the book. There have been times when I hoped that they hadn't.'

They all looked at him with some surprise.

'Yes, I mean it,' he went on. 'You and I wrote what we thought was right at the time, but when the years have passed and you see all the meanings that people can read into what you have written, and how misguided you were to have written some things at all – it makes you think.'

'But I was right in the book I followed. The book Karl Marx wrote, and which was my Bible.' Stalin said. 'We looked at society and saw that it was corrupt and rotten. We saw the barriers that cut off country from country and man from man: tariff walls, national interests, monopolies of raw materials, language, tradition, religion – especially religion. We saw that there were low places in these walls.'

'Such as?' Hitler asked, in a tone that seemed to imply that the way to world government was the way of bombs and panzers.

'Such as medicine,' Stalin explained, 'and art, and science, and literature. If men could cross the barriers in pursuit of these, they could cross all barriers.'

'Because they had a common interest, you mean?' Moses asked.

Stalin said, 'Exactly,' and thumped the table with his big fist. 'And we saw that the greatest common interest was among the wage slaves.'

'That's everybody,' said Paul, and winked at Moses. Stalin went on. 'Why shouldn't the wage slaves break down the barriers, and reach out the hand of friendship in a chain round the whole world?'

'Nonsense!' Hitler looked as if he would like to spit.

'If that's nonsense, Adolph, what makes sense?' Stalin's heavy brows were down. He was out for an argument.

'My way,' said Hitler, and stood up. He was the kind of man who talked better on his feet. 'The world is not made for the weak; it is made for the strong. You'll never get anywhere if you wait for the lame and the halt and the blind. The unfit must stand aside and take their chance. The whole purpose and point in the evolution of man is to produce the super man, who is in every sense as superior to ordinary humanity as ordinary humanity is to the brute beast. Everything must be sacrificed to that: every human value that religion and philosophy have preached and thought. Every human decency must be sacrificed if it stands in the way of the purpose. The superman must be.' He sat down and seemed surprised that there was no applause.

Paul looked at the ceiling. 'I wonder,' he said, almost to himself. 'I wonder what came unstuck.'

'So do I, Paul,' Moses looked into the fire.

'I'll tell you,' Stalin growled. 'Human nature. We thought we would lead a crusade for the working class: each man ready to sacrifice, suffer, and die for the sake of the cause, and we found that the average working man was more concerned with filling in a football coupon in the hope that he might become a capitalist, than he was with making himself a good socialist. We found that men sweat and toil, not for the sake of society, but for their own sakes, and the sake of their wives and families. One day men complain that they are being exploited, and next day when the chance is given, they are first to exploit their fellows. They'll joyfully take the last shilling off a fellow at pontoon, they'll work overtime when others are unemployed – I just can't understand it.'

'I can,' said Hitler grimly, 'And it bears out what I've just been saying. Ordinary people are no use. The world exists for the best, not for the worst. What you need is a leader who makes up his mind what is required and goes for it, and keeps going for it through hell and high water. Ein Reich, ein volk, ein Fuehrer. That's the recipe. Don't let anything stand in your way. Use any means: murder, lies, intrigue, terror. It doesn't matter. The end justifies the means; the strong man's place is at the top.'

'The top of what?' Paul asked innocently.

'The top of the world. King of the castle.' He paused as if expecting applause again. All he got was an 'Oh' from Moses, and an 'Ah' from Paul. And then Paul said quietly.

'And why didn't you get there, Adolph?'

Hitler sat down abruptly, looking somewhat deflated.

'I don't know,' he groaned. 'I just don't know. But we were the greatest people on earth; by every law of God and man we were. To dominate mankind was our destiny.'

Moses looked at Paul. 'Shall I tell them?' he asked. Paul sighed and said yes: he had done it so often it wearied him.

'Listen you two,' Moses began, and there was the ring of authority in his voice. 'Listen and don't interrupt while I tell you one or two home truths.'

They recognized the authority and did not interrupt. Moses went on.

'The first thing the two of you have got to get into your heads, is that you're not anything special. Paul and I have passed dozens like you through our hands. I've seen more than Paul for I've been here longer. There was a fellow who didn't want to be separated from his horse. Genghis Khan was his name; and a compatriot of your old pal Mussolini, Adolph; chap called Julius Caesar. Little fellow with thin hair who wore a laurel wreath to hide the bald bit.'

'Remember that other nordic type, Moses,' Paul interrupted. 'We had an awful time with him: Attila the Hun, wasn't it? And the short stout character, the Frenchman, what was his name again?'

'Napoleon,' Moses smiled reminiscently. 'Yes, they were all here, with all the philosophers who proved to their own satisfaction that there isn't anything here. We had Marx and Lenin and Trotsky, Joseph. They all came and they all went.'

'Where?' Stalin asked, a trifle nervously I thought.

'Through that door,' Paul nodded sideways.

'But I thought . . .' Hitler began.

'Yes, you thought,' and there was a trace of impatience in the way Moses said it. 'You thought, but you didn't think hard enough or long enough. Nobody ever does. I didn't, Paul didn't. I led my people for forty years to a promised land and what happened?'

'They lost it,' Hitler sneered. 'But I will say they're doing better now. More unity, more guts. Better leadership if I may say so. They could have done it in the old days too, if they'd had more faith in their star.'

'No, that wasn't it,' said Paul. 'It wasn't that they hadn't enough faith in the true star. Their trouble was that they had too much faith in the wrong star. They got carried away by the idea that they were the people; there was nobody like them. Why, even I was convinced of that at one time, till I learned more sense.'

Moses nodded. 'Yes, everything we did was right. It had to be right simply because we did it. We were the chosen people. We had a destiny.'

'Indeed we had,' said Paul. 'The trouble was that we didn't realise what our destiny was.'

'You had no leader,' Hitler growled. 'Without a leader you get nowhere.'

'You're wrong, Adolph,' said Paul very quietly. 'My people did have a dedicated leader, the most dedicated leader that any nation ever had.'

'You mean Jesus?' Hitler scoffed. 'How could that decadent weakling ever lead anything? With his degenerate philosophy. The stuff he dished out was pap for babies, not meat for men.'

'I'm not so sure,' said Stalin slowly, puffing away at his cold pipe. 'No, I'm not so sure. Jesus' ideas were right enough, after all they were communist ideas. It was his method that was wrong. You must have political action. Evolution is too slow; you must have revolution if you're going to see change in your time.'

Moses slowly and sadly shook his great head.

'You are two foolish men. Very foolish men. Can't you see, Adolph Hitler, that it was this very Jesus who brought you crashing to the ground and dragged you back from the borders of your promised land? Can't you see, Joseph Stalin, that you cannot begin to justify the brotherhood of man till you accept the fatherhood of God? You followed your stars, both of you. But they were the wrong stars.'

'Yes, friends,' said Paul. 'There is only one way which leads to the top, every other road ends on the brink of the abyss. And there is only one star which leads men by that road.'

'What star?' Hitler sneered.

'A star,' said Paul with a smile, 'that shone in a promised land over a stable where the promise was kept.'

'I don't believe it.' Hitler snapped.

'I wonder,' Stalin whispered.

'Well, you'll know in a minute.' Paul rose and stretched himself. 'For the door is opening.'

'But I thought it couldn't open.' Hitler was nervous.

'I didn't think there was anything on the other side.' Stalin put his pipe in his pocket and rubbed his sweating palms down the seam of his trousers.

'Ah,' said Moses, with a twinkle in his eye. 'But it does open; and there is something.'

'What is there?' Stalin asked, after he had swallowed the lump in his throat.

'Understanding,' said Moses in a kindly way. 'Just understanding.'

Hitler was moving towards the open door as if he was hypnotized. Then he stopped and turned.

'But aren't you going through too?'

'No, Adolph,' Paul smiled. 'We have been through. Our job is to stay here, waiting.'

'Waiting for what?' Stalin asked.

'Waiting for the millions of others who will come by the same roads that you have come by and finish at that same door.'

So Adolph Hitler and Joseph Stalin passed through the doorway, and it closed behind them with the firmness of finality.

And Paul looked at Moses and Moses looked at Paul, who smiled and shrugged his shoulders. And they both sighed and sat down a little wearily by the fire waiting for the next arrival. Who might be you; and who might be me.

Two Days To Christmas

THIS was a Christmas Broadcast on BBC television. The Sunday must have come in on the 23rd of December, which makes it a wee bit awkward, for people aren't quite in the Christmas mood. There's still the odd present to get, and of course you've just got time to send off the Christmas card to the folk you forgot to send one to but who haven't forgotten to send one to you, and who won't be put off with a New Year card.

Two days to Christmas: that was the title I gave to the broadcast, because it happened to be two days to Christmas. And the thought came to me, that there must have been a day which was two days from the first Christmas, and that all the folk who were involved in what happened at Christmas, and in what happened because there was Christmas, must have been doing something that day. I used my imagination, and wondered what they were doing. But first, I had to get the viewers interested, with the help, of course, of the producer and the studio crew. I began this way.

Two days from Christmas, and all these things to be got, and the last pay day gone.

There's no use asking you what you're doing at this particular juncture, for if you're watching me you're watching the Telly.

If you are male, your wife is probably asking what you are doing watching that thing (and I hope she's not referring to me) when there's all these parcels to be parcelled, and all these cards to be addressed, 'With Love', when you could see them far enough, and you wouldn't be sending them a card at all if they hadn't sent you one last year, which they did only because they had an extra one, and couldn't think of anybody else.

And if you are a female and married, your man is probably opening the door and saying, 'It's all very well for you sitting there and watching Dow on the Telly, but what's aunt Jessie's address?'

Yes, it's two days to Christmas, and the house is the usual shambles, apart from the blood. For that's the way things go, two days from Christmas, and the things we say about our friends and relations just don't fall into the category of peace on earth, goodwill towards men. Our consolation is that they are probably saying the same about us.

Here's Joseph and Mary two days before Christmas, and Mary hasn't very long to go. A lot of you know what Mary and Joseph were thinking then, for you can forget about miracles; here was a young wife expecting her first, and here was her man, and the man is usually more nervous than the woman.

Two days to go, and still to get from Nazareth to Bethlehem, and you folk with a family know what it's like, two days to go. There's maybe some of you who are only two days away from the everlasting miracle of birth, and you'll be hoping – of course you'll be hoping, that the baby will be born on Christmas day. If it's a boy he'll be Noel, if it's a girl she'll be Carol.

They know that there's an inn at Bethlehem, but they're not booked in. Maybe there'll be no room, Joseph is thinking as he trudges on leading the donkey which carries Mary.

And of course there was an inn at Bethlehem, the best known caravanserai in all the world, that will be known to the end of time for one thing, and for one thing only: that when Mary and Joseph knocked on the door, they couldn't get in.

But it was there all right, two days before Christmas. Some inns glory in being able to advertise that Queen Elizabeth slept here; or that the Duke of Wellington slept here. Though one boarder commented that it was no wonder he was known as the Iron Duke. Or, in Scotland, that Robert Burns slept here. But the proprietor of the Bethlehem inn never for a moment thought that the fame of his inn would rest on the fact that Jesus did not sleep here.

Yes, they can deck the place up and ornament it and elaborate it, and make pilgrimages to it, but the inn doesn't matter. It's people who matter. And here's a man, mine host of Bethlehem, rubbing his hands tonight for he's never had a week like this, and not knowing that in two days' time he's going to join the immortals for the wrong reason.

Of course he wasn't the only one. Joseph and Mary and the donkey are coming slowly down the rough road from Nazareth, and away out there in the desert, three astrologers are following a star. Two days from the end of the trail, with gold and frankincense and myrrh. Not knowing what they were going to find, and not knowing what they would do with it when they found it.

And in the end of the day, two days later, all they could think of doing was to bend the knee and leave their presents, and head away back home.

And shepherds too, abiding in the fields. It's easy enough to know what they were doing two days from Christmas. They were doing what they had been doing two years before Christmas. They were minding their sheep, not knowing that in forty-eight hours they would be in company with the angels, and in company with one a lot more important than all the angels put together: with Jesus, the Saviour of the world.

And there's Augustus Caesar, away over the sea in imperial Rome, sleeping as soundly as it is possible for a Roman Emperor who calls himself a god, to sleep.

He's about 43 or 44 by this time. He has won everything his uncle Julius had dreamed about when he crossed the Rubicon. Cassius is dead, and Brutus is dead, and Mark Antony is dead, and even Cleopatra is dead. He is lord of the earth, and for the first time for centuries, his empire is at peace.

He has ordered a census; he wants to know exactly how many live under his rule. Of course he knows that the census cannot be exact. Old people will have died between the time they were counted and the time they were registered. Babies will be born after the count is made. He doesn't know how many babies. He thinks it doesn't very much matter. But it does matter. A baby will be born in faraway, troublesome Judea, in two days' time, and in the reign of Tiberius that baby will be crucified on a hill called Calvary, and that 400 years later that cross would be emblazoned on the burnished shields of imperial Rome.

Of course he couldn't know, could he? It was still two days to Christmas.

And here's an oldish woman dandling her baby on her knee. A wee bit old to have a baby, mind you. A stranger might be excused for thinking she was the boy's grannie. But no, he is her own, and her only son. It has happened before and it will no doubt happen again. Her name is Elizabeth, and she has called the baby, John.

She knows her cousin Mary's baby must be just about due now. Not any more than a day or two, and she's not jealous of Mary or of Mary's baby when the baby is born. And that wee boy cradled on her knees will not be jealous either, when thirty years on he comes out of the wilderness and the people flock to him, and, hearing him, ask if he is the Messiah. Maybe he will be tempted to say that he is, and he will certainly fit the picture the people have of what a Messiah ought to be like.

But no. He will tell them that his cousin is the Messiah, the very Lamb of God

And John does not know (how could he?) and Elizabeth does not know (how could she?) that in a school for the Roman aristocracy there is a boy called Herod, son of the tetrarch, a man of complicated family life with a number of wives and a large family, and not very sure whose mother is which.

Two days before Christmas he was reasonably happy; he'd had many rivals for the throne but he'd managed one way or another to get rid of most of them. He was a wee bit worried, though, at the tale these Persian astrologers were telling him two days before Christmas. But not greatly worried. Here was a situation which could be cleared up without any bother.

He didn't know it, but he wasn't going to live very long after Christmas. He didn't know that he had failed to get rid of the danger. Just as his son did not know that one day he would order the death of Elizabeth's son, John, and the name of Herod would stink forever in the nostrils of mankind.

And here's a dozen men going about their lawful occasions around Galilee. Two days before Christmas they were just boys, a couple of them hadn't even been born then. But this is what they had become. Andrew, that good Scot, and his brother Peter, James and John, quiet enough living men who were to become the sons of thunder. Philip and Bartholomew and Nathaniel; Matthew, an inland revenue type; Thomas, the twin, and, of course Judas Iscariot himself, poor soul.

The fame or infamy of these twelve men begins when the boy who will be born two days from now, comes out of Nazareth to Galilee.

And here is Pontius Pilate himself. Son of a wealthy freed slave. He'll be about 20 or 21, two days before Christmas, for Jesus was 25 when Pilate succeeded Valerius Gratus as procurator of Judea. I don't know what he was doing two days from Christmas. Maybe nothing of very much importance. He was an ambitious man. He would like to be a famous man. So he will be, so indeed he will be.

They're all here two days from Christmas, waiting for their cue and ready to step on to the stage and play their part in the tremendous drama that is building up, and will build up for another thirty-three years. They all have their part to play.

Caiaphas – he'll be about 30 – and his old father-in-law, Annas. They weren't bothering about what was happening down in the city of David. Why should they? It was no concern of theirs. It couldn't possibly make any difference to their way of life.

And a wee shilpit cratur by the name of Saul. His parents were worried about him. They thought they might lose him. He's about five years old two days before Christmas, and already he's doing very well at school in the Greek city of Tarsus. They reckon he's got a future, their delicate son Saul. So he has. Here's one who in thirty years' time will have changed more than his name, which will be Paul.

And there's others, some yet unborn, who will become real people because of what was to happen in two days from now.

A woman taken in adultery, which, God help us, is not of all sins the most deadly. A wee man who will sit on the branch of a tree to see over the heads of the others. Zaccheus is his name. A young man called Nicodemus who will want to know how a man can be born again, and will be told by the one who will be born two days from now.

A farmer who built bigger barns and who was the only one whom Jesus called a fool.

And there's one who, two days before Christmas, was a wild young rip of a lad who the neighbours said would come to a bad end.

So he did; the worst end of all. Nailed to a cross, and whose last words were spoken to another man on a cross, 'When you come into your kingdom, remember me.'

They leap out and live and have become immortal because of what they thought of that baby to be born in two days time.

What do we think of him, you and I? We have two days to make up our minds.

On Christmas Eve will we listen with the children, and maybe we will catch the echo of the angel song.

Call him Son of Man; call him Son of God; it does not matter in the slightest. For the baby who will be born two days from now changed the world and nobody can deny it.

This birth has something to do with you, and there are still two days to decide what it is. Think on it, pray about it, and the night after tomorrow night kneel down with the wise men who are the simple men, and wait till Christ is born.

THOUGHT FOR THE DAY
21st - 25th January, 1974

<u>MONDAY</u>

AYE Aye. Douglas Aitken spiered gin I wad tak' Thought for Today this week, I jaloused that he had a notion at the back o' his mind. And sae he had. For he had minded that this is Burns week, when a' kinds o' gaitherins tak' place, frae the Lunnon Caledonian Society's tae the Drumtochty Kirk o' Scotland Weemin's Guils, when they eat the sacramental haggis and drink the Immortal Memory in various beverages frae John Barleycorn tae lemonade.

Though aiblins the year there's some o'the cooks that are gey worried about a power cut afore the haggis is ready, for there's naething mair scunnorsome than cauld haggis, unless cauld tatties and cauld neeps. And the three o' them cauld the gither is eneuch tae mak' ony mortal grue, excep' them that mean what they say when they say they could eat a horse.

But a thought for the day canna just be aboot Burns, or hauf the population wad switch aff their sets, syne for ene that hauds up Burns as an example, there's anither that houds him doon as a warnin'.

I couldna say eneuch guid about Burns tae suit some, and I couldna say eneuch ill about Burns tae suit the ithers.

D'ye mind Carmichael in *Beside the Bonnie Brier Bush?* He's comin' out for a meenister, but afore he finishes his mither dies, and her last words tae him were, 'Aye put in a guid word for Christ.'

I wad be fause tae my callin' and tae the chance their meenits gie me, gin I didna dae the same.

Mind ye, there's them that wad ca' it blasphemy tae speak o' the twa o' them thegither, thinkin' it means that I consider them tae hae been the same type o' men. And Guid kens that's faur frae the truth. But they had a common humanity, and that's what I want tae speak about. Sae we'll look at some words that Burns wrote, and some words that Jesus spak, and see gin they hae a common sough. And see gin atween them they can tell us what could be for our help and for our guid.

And wi' your leave (or e'en without your leave) I'll tik' a wee liberty wi' scripture.

In his Epistle to John Lapraik Burns writes o' himsel'.

> I am nae poet in a sense,
> But juist a rhymenr, like, by chance;
> And hae tae learning nae pretence,
>> Yet what the matter?
> When e'er my Muse does on me glance,
>> I jingle at her.

Burns was ower modest when he wrote that, for he was a poet, and a very guid ane. The words might fit me better that has a habit o' stroning things up in rhyme; and this is the liberty I'll tak wi' Haly Writ. First, then Burns in his first Epistle to Davie.

> It's no'in titles nor in rank,
> It's no' in wealth like Lunnon bank,
> To purchase peace and rest.
> It's no' in makin' muckle mair,
> It's no' in books, it's no' in lear,
> To mak' us truly blest.
> If happiness hae not her seat
> And centre in the breast,
> We may be wise, or rich, or great,
> But never can be blest.
> Nae treasures nor pleasures
> Could mak' us happy lang.
> The heart aye's the part aye,
> That maks us richt or wrang.

Now the Lord Jesus:

> Disciples ye are and guid men a';
> Ye followed nae kennin' whaurawa'
> Ye might be led, or what might befa'
> Afore the en'.
> Now come ye speirin' me about wha
> Will be greatest then.
> Ye see this bit lad that I haud by the han'
> Gin ye dinna change, aye ilka man
> And end as simple as ye began,
> Wi' the heart o' a bairn'

41

Ye'll ne'er see the kingdom. Ye understan'?
Ye'll get your fairin'.
What dae ye mean by bein' great?
The Kingdom's nae that sort o' state.
God's wisdom't nae sophisticate.
And ye will find,
There's juist ae greatness that they rate
A childlike mind.

TUESDAY

THERE'S a bit o' agy-bargy gaes on about what tae the day and the hour, and e'en tae the year, the Lord Jesus was born. But there's a kind o' consensus of opinion, backit up by Roman history, and by some excursions in astronomy about some conjunction o' Jupiter and Saturn, that wad seem tae place his birthday in the year seven BC, which sounds a wee bit odd. And the day in the month o' December suits well eneuch syne the auld warld held holiday when the shortest day was by and men lookit tae the sun comin' back again.

There's nae doubt about Burns' birthday, for he tak's note o't himsel', and disnae juist leave it tae the parish records.

Our monarch's hindmost year but one
Was five and twenty days begun'
'Twas then a blast o' Janwar win'
Blew hansel in on Robin.

The monarch was George the second, son o' the wee wee German laidie, and the year was 1759, juist fourteen year eftir Culloden.

There were nae records in Jesus' day of course, excep' that it was a census that brought a' the Davidson's tae Bethlehem, and naebody kens gin the new born bairn was counted in or out.

Aiblins it didna mean muckle tae them at the time, but there's nae birth in a human time has meant mair tae the warld than that ane.

For ane there was nae room in the inn. For the ither there was a house that his faither had biggit wi' his ain hauns; an' the nicht Robert was born, the gable end blew in. We've a' had a taste o' Janwar winds this year. And they had tae hap Robert up in the cloots they had, and carry him tae a neebor.

It's an odd thing – though, Guid forgie us it's nae a' that odd – that when there's a prophet born that naebody wants, it seems that the warld itsel' disna want him either.

For the warld juist disna want onybody that disturbs its peace: that shakes us out o' our complacencies, and maks us think.

Naebody wants tae think. It's faur mair congenial for tae sit back and let ither folk dae the thinkin', nae matter how ill-thought that thinkin' may be.

Burns was born intae, a strict upbrining. It was Calvinist. And in some weys he didna like it. It didna like him muckle either. He put his opinion o't intil the mouth o' Holy Wille Fisher. I'm sorry I canna gie ye the hale thing. Twa verses will suffice.

> O Thou wha in the heavens dost dwell.
> Wha as it pleases best Thysel'
> Sends ane to Heaven and ten tae hell
> A' for Thy glory.
> And no' for ony guid or ill
> They've dune afore Thee.
>
> But Lord, remember me and mine,
> Wi' mercies temporal and divine,
> That I for fear and grace may shine
> Excelled by nane.
> And a' the glory shall be Thine.
> Amen. Amen.

That's Calvanism at its worst and as it was misunderstood in the Scotland of Burns. But he could see behind the sham. In his dedication to his friend and patron Gavin Hamilton he wrote:

> O ye wha leave the springs o' Calvin
> For gumlie dubs o' your ain delvin'
> Ye sons o' heresy and error,
> Ye'll someday squeal in quakin' terror.

Jesus was a Calvinist, though he lived long afore Calvin, He had the thocht that what's for ye'll nae gae by ye. Whilk isna an ill thought tae have.

And when the manheid was drainin' out o' him in the gairden, and his smedum was gey near spent, this he minded o':

> The Lord went out tae Gethsemane,
> Wi' Peter and the sons o' Zebedee,
> To collogue wi' God – Is it me or Thee?
> What div ye think?
> This bitter cup ye haud out to me,
> Am I tae drink?

Is this the fate I wad hae forsweired?
Maun I gae on and dree my weird?
Faither, dear Faither, aft hae I speired
Wad ye no' bethink?
O faither dear, your son is feared
This cup tae drink.

Sae Jesus prayed neath the Paschal mune,
O Faither' gin it's tae be my boon
Tae dance my days tae your new tune,
I'm in your keepin'.
And eftir the Lord's sae sair commune,
He fand them sleepin'

WEDNESDAY

YE'LL aibline be thinkin' that the Tocht for the day, the week, has sae far nae been a' that cheery. And aibline ye're richt but, ye see, I canna tell juist what wey ye're feelin' this mornin' and I think ye'll agree that it's folk that arena feelin' juist as cheery as they micht be that need the word mair than them that's life is gaen like a weel gaun mill.

There wad be bairns born in the nicht: it's but a fortnight syne the wife and me had anither granwean, and that maks fower a' thegither. How our giud daughter was feelin' I can jalouse, but I dinna hae tae speculate on how our son was feelin', for I've been through this mysel'. It taks an awfu' lot out a man.

So there's plenty are feelin' grand this mornin', and ane or twa that are no, because things didna gang weel at a'.

But gin I've tae choose atween one mood and anither, I think ye'll agree I should hae a word for them that's feelin' doon and dowie the day, for they need it mair nor the ithers. Think about them, friens. Folk that hae been up a' nicht because there's sickness in the, hoose. Folk that hae taen their last fareweel o' ane that's dear til them; and guid kens there's plenty o' them.

When Burns was in his last illness doon in Dumfries (and gin he'd had a better doctor he wadnae hae been in extremis) Jean Armour his faithfu' and forgien' wife couldna tend him as she wad hae wanted for she was about tae be brocht tae bed wi' anither bairn. The bairn was born on the verra day Burns was buried; and there's a pathetic thing for ye.

But there was ane that served him weel. Her name was Jessie Lewars, and Burns wrote one o' his best sangs for her, a sang that Mendelssohn put music to, that fits the words real weel.

> O wert thou in the cauld blast,
> On yonder lea, on yonder lea.
> My plaidie tae the angry airt,
> I'd shelter thee, I'd shelter thee.
> Or should misfortune's bitter blast
> Aroun' thee blaw, aroun' thee blaw.
> Thy bield wad be my bosom,
> Tae share it a', tae share it a'.
>
> Or were I in the wildest waste,
> Sae black and bare, sae black and bare;
> The desert were a paradise,
> If thou wert there, if thou wert there.
> Or were I monarch of the globe,
> With thee to reign, with thee to reign,
> The brightest jewel in my crown,
> Wad be my queen; wad be my queen.

What we've been daen in these wee talks, is tae find a word o' Burns and a word o' the Lord Jesus that say the same thing; and of course, it's nae easy tae find a word o' the Lord Jesus that says juist this, for as far as lassies gae, and ither delights tae, the Lord Jesus and Robert Burns were twa verra different men, though when I think o' Jesus and weemin I aye think o' that house at Bethany and Jesus' frien' Lazarus that had twa sisters, Mary and Martha that didn't get on a' that weel, and I hae a notion that the reason they didna get on a that weel is that baith o' them were in luve wi' the Lord, and what wey ho'? Is there ony reason why a woman should fa' in luve wi' Robert Burns, and nane fa' in luve wi' the Lord?

And aiblins Jesus kenned it; and sae, maybe, did Lazarus. But that's juist in the passin', but it's a thocht nane the less. And whaur will we look for a word o' the Lord that's the same word that Burns penned for Jessie Lewars.

We'll turn tae paraphrase 43, whilk is frae St John in chapter 14.

> Sune ye'll hear my voice nae mair
> This aye has been my fate.
> But I promise ye, and speak ye fair,
> Ye'll hae your advocate.

When I'm nae wi' ye, ye will ken
I'm wi' my faither dear;
But bide a wee, and ye'll sune ken
I'm here, my friend, I'm here.

The ties that bind us here on earth
Are still there when we dee;
There's life in daith as weel's in birth:
Your deid still live in me.

What the warld gies, friens, gie not I
And my giving wilna cease;
I gie ye now till eternity,
I gie ye a' my peace.

THURSDAY

NOW we meet twa men wha ken that their end is near. Burns is sick and he kens he's sick: he's dying and he kens he's dying.

Of course he had aye been a bit feared o' death had Burns, and he'd thought about it mair than a normal healthy man wad. He was, in fact, a bit morbid, was Burns. But then, frae he was a lad, he never kenned what was wrang wi' him. Neither did onybody else, and why should they, for rheumatic fever had never been discovered in his day. But that was his trouble, and he'd had a hard life o't tryin' tae mak' a leevin out o' barren acres.

And mind ye' Burns was a grand fermer, and he and his brither Gilbert were fermers fare afore their time.

In 1783 the Glesca Mercury reported that 'Robert Burns, Lochlea Farm, Tarbolton Parish had won a prize o' three pun' for lintseed saved for sawin'. That was for growin' the flax or the crop in the next year. But they never made a success o't. But he started off tae be a poet.

This ane. *In Prospect of Death* isna ane o' his best or his brightest, and I'll nae gie ye it a', for it's nae worth it. But it gies ye an inklin o' his mood.

O Thou unknown Almighty cause.
Of all my hope and fear;
In whose dread presence ere an hour,
Perhaps I may appear.

Where with intention I have erred
No other plea I have;
But Thou art good, and goodness still
Delighteth to forgive.

What made Burns feel, that he was near to death is a matter of speculation.

A lot of moderns eftir a Burns supper have wished that they were deid, but are still in the land o' the leevin'. But somehow or anither, the thocht o' daith was aye in Burns' mind. For example tak' *Man was Made to Mourn.*

O man! Wha in the early years
How prodigal o' time.
Misspending all they precious hours
Thy glorious youthful prime.
Alternate follies take the sway
Licentious passions burn;
While tenfold force gives nature's law
That man was made to mourn.

See yonder poor o'erlaboured wight
So abject, mean and vile,
Who begs a brother of the earth
To give him leave to toil.
And see his lordly fellow worm
The poor petition spurn;
Unmindful though a weeping wife
And helpless offspring mourn.

O Death, the poor man's dearest friend,
The kindliest and the best;
Welcome the hour my aged limbs
Are laid with thee at rest.
The great, the wealthy, fear thy blow,
From pomp and pleasure torn.
But O! A blest relief to those
That weary laden, mourn.

Noo we'll think o' the ither, for Burns was feeling gey low, and wha hasna? Let's think o' the ither that hadna a place tae lay his head, and wha kent real weel that frae the meenit he cam' through Jerusalem gate on the cuddy's back, he was ridin' by the Messiah's road till his daith.

Here's anither man, front faced wi' daith, and sure he was sick, and sure he was sorry.

I'll paraphrase a paraphrase, that we a' sing afore the sacrament, and that aiblins we dinna think o' as we micht,

> This was the nicht when Jesus did ken
> That they'd have their will, the hatefu' men,
> They were at their supper afore the misdeed,
> And the saviour o' the warld brak' bread.
> He stood a whiley, aye, he stood a wee,
> And he gied the guid Lord his gramercy;
> Then in his hauns he brak the breid
> And said til the twal', Noo lads, tak' heed
> What I've done tae the scone they will dae tae me,
> My body they'll brak when they crucifee.
> We're a' bund doon wi' an earthly shackle
> But sune I'll be free frae my tabernacle.
> And ilk nicht when ye come tae your supper table
> Ye'll mind o' this nicht as faur as ye're able
> And mind o' the day when I first woo'ed ye,
> And then ye'll ken how muckle I loo'ed ye.
> Then our Lord, maist weary did stoop
> And in his hauns he took the stroup
> This, my frien's for your lasting guid'
> This my frien's, just means my bluid,

There's twa weys o' facing death. I think the Lord's wey the better.

FRIDAY

THERE'S mony a sang o' Burns has been sung ower the last couple o' weeks, just according to the taste o' the singer. But there's ane that has bee sung at a' the gaitherin's and for a surety that ane's Auld Lang Syne, the Americans and ithers that haena had the privilege of a Scottish education ca' it Auld Lang Zyne.

Naebody kens wha wrote it, but it wasna Burns. He heard it frae an auld man and he wrote it down, and when he sent it to Mrs Dunlop he wrote:

'Light be the turf on the breast of the heaven-inspired poet who wrote this glorious fragment. There is more of the fire of native guid in it than in half a dozen of modern English Bacchanalians.'

And I may say in the passing that there will be a queer lot of versions of Auld Lang Syne that will be sung the night, that werena' written by Burns either.

Should auld acquaintance be forgot,
And never brought to min'
Should auld acquaintance be forgot
And auld lang syne.

For auld lang syne my dear,
For auld lang syne,
We'll tak' a cup o' kindness yet
For auld lang syne.

And there's a hand my trusty fiere
And gie's a hand o' thine
And we'll tak' a richt guid-willie waught
For auld lang syne.

For auld lang syne my dear
For auld lang syne
We'll tak' a cup o' kindness yet
For auld lang syne.

It's a sentimental sang of course, but then we Scots are a sentimental folk though we pretend we're no'. We pretend were a' hard headed folk wha aye hae their e'e on the practicalities o' livin'. But we're onything but, whilk is ae reason for a' the Burns celebrations that are gaen on at this time o' year.

Wi' the best will in the warld the English couldna grow sentimental ower William Shakespeare, they wouldna' even think o' callin' him Willie.

I may be wrang, but I dinna think I'm wrang tae hae in my mind a picture o' the Last Supper wi' the Twal', or it wad iust be the eleven, for Judas had gane awa' tae dae what he was tae dae, standin' roun' the table, airms across and hand grippin' hand as only the hands o' auld frien's can grip. The wey ye tak' hans when ane o' ye's gane awa' and ye dinna ken gin ye'll see him again.

Aiblins this isna what the disciples were thinkin', but it was surely what Jesus was thinkin' that nicht.

On Monday I said I wad tak' some lilerties wi' Haly Writ, tho' I felt there were some that nicht tak' exception tae it. But there's nae need.

The men that wrote the Metrical psalms that are sae dear til us did that, and sae did the men that wrote the paraphrases.

Sae what I've dune the day is tae tak' ane o' the paraphrases that we dinna sing a' that often, and just tae gie ye a Scots sough; Paraphrase 429; the words our Lord has recorded in the fourteenth o' St John: and this is Jesus' Auld Lang Syne.

Now dinna let your hear be feared
Wi' tribble or dismay;
It's a' been changed syne I appeared
Juist listen tae what I say.

I'm gaen awa back tae my faither's hame
Whaur there's a place for me;
And nae for me alane: the same
Is waitin there for ye.

But I maun gae afore ye there
Tae put the place in trim;
I'm still your auld frien', ye'll nae despair
Ye'll be hame wi' me and him.

When your day comes, and it's nae here yet,
I'll come back and gie ye a cry;
Our auld acquaintance ye'll no' forget
Auld friend, and ne'er will I.

We've been thegither three year back
And mony an unco hae seen,
We've had mony a ploy and mony a crack.
It will be as it aye has been.

For I am the way, the life, the truth
And tae God ye canna come
Til ye risk the cross and the town's Tolbooth
And the hale Palladium.

Let's take the risk you and me.

FISHERMAN'S TALE

GALILEE loch lies blue to the sun,
And ringed around by the sand-brown hill;
And over the water when day is done
The fisherman's boat comes homeward still.
While the sea grows dark in the loom of the land,
And the wee waves speak on the shingle shore.
Then the lamp is lit by the goodwife's hand,
And the fisherman bends his back to the oar,
And the ripples spread from the thrusting prow.
A lamp in a window, a boatie at sea.
So it was then, and so it is now.
Well I remember, said old Zebedee.

Aye, well I remember that night in the gloaming
Well I remember the lamplight that shone;
Well I remember the three of us homing,
Myself and my laddies, young Jamie and John.
We'd been out since the dawn, we were famished and wet;
The loch had been angry, the fishing was bad;
The sail had been split and we'd near lost our net;
And John had been sick; he's a delicate lad.
We beached her, and shouldered the oars and the mast,
And came up over the shingle the laddies and me;
The longest and weariest day ends at last.
Well I remember, said old Zebedee.

The fellow was set at the side of the road,
Just out of the lamplight beside the front door.
I might have passed by with a word and a nod,
But I said to myself, 'I have seen you before.'
The laddies both stopped, and they set down their gear;
You cannot be looking for friends in this place,
Where there's none but the wife and the laddies and me.'
He turned, and the lamplight fell full on his face.
Well I remember, said old Zebedee.

I had seen him before, I had thought, you'll keep mind;
Now I knew where and when I had seen.
For the joys and the sorrows of all humankind
Were alive and alight in his e'en.
The weal and the woe, and the hopes and the fears,
Never were two eyes like yon.
I felt my own eyes stinging salt with my tears,
I looked over to Jamie and John.
John was as white as yon gowan flower;
Jamie was red as is yon rowan tree.
I saw that my laddies had come to their hour.
Well I remember, said old Zebedee.

I blinked, and I swallowed the lump in my throat;
'Is your business with me, then,' said I?
'We're wearied with fishing all day in the boat;
If there's something you want, come in by.
We're starved, and we're cold, and there's meat in the pot,
And a place for yourself at the board.'
I sounded off hand, but I knew for all that,
This was the day of the Lord.
He reached out his hands to my laddies, and then,
With his eyes full of pity he turned them on me.
'They're mine and I'll make of them fishers of men.'
Well I remember, said old Zebedee.

I turned away then, and I went to the door;
I swithered a minute, the latch in my hand,
'You must speak to their mother, and tell her before
We can go any further, you must understand.'
When the supper was by, I says, 'Sir, it's but right
You should tell why you want them, and when.
You meet us outby in the mirk of the night
And you talk about fishers of men.
These two are good lads though I say it mysel'
And we work well together, we three,
So off hand and straight now your tale you must tell.'
Well I remember, said old Zebedee.

Maybe you've had your long dreams, lang, lang syne,
Before this sour world with its care
Drove them out of your heart, as the world did with mine,
And your hopes and your dreams you forswear.
Maybe you've dreamed of a world pleased with peace,
Where all folk were neighbours, and kind.
When the wars and the rumours of wars would all cease;
A world where a poor man might find
A home and a hearthplace; a table well spread;
For his honest day's work a fair fee;
Well, all that you've dreamed of and prayed for, he said.
Well I remember, said old Zebedee.

I looked over at Jamie, and over at John,
And I saw what was there to be seen.
They were his to the death I could see after yon;
And their mother was wiping her e'en.
But I thought, and I said to myself, 'Does she ken
What may hap to the bairns that she bore?
Does she think that this Gospel he's bearing to men
Will win through, when all gospels before
Are despised and rejected by sinful men's scorn?
Will Jesus's way not go agee,
Till Jamie and John curse the day they were born?'
Well I remember, said old Zebedee.

Then I said 'I'll not counter the will of my God;
And what a man wins he may tyne,
These laddies of mine, they can take their own road.'
But, 'No' Jesus says. 'They'll take mine.'
'And where will that take them to,' asks the good wife?
Says Jesus, 'I do not right ken;
But a kingdom there is, and eternal's the life,
What more do you want for your men?'
I saw this had pleased her; 'A kingdom?' she said.
'Then happy am I to agree.'
Said I, 'Wait till the morning: we should all be in bed.'
Well I remember, said old Zebedee.

In the morning they went, the two laddies and him.
And left me to fish all alone.
And I thought they might sink and I thought they might swim
But it was not the same with them gone.
And the years went by, and there came a day
When the goodwife went after her two;
She said that this Jesus was long with the pay;
That the crown and the kingdom were long overdue.
And I was alone, If we all had our wish
And nobody sailed on the sea,
I doubt they'd go hungry, man, wanting the fish.
Well I remember, said old Zebedee.

One day there came rumour the new song was sung;
Jesus was dead; in his grave.
The tale of the wonderful gospel had run
To the same hinder end as the lave.
Prophets should fish, then they would not forget
What the fishing can teach you right weel;
That it's easy enough whiles to cast out your net,
But casting may not fill your creel.
Never was prophet or saint on the earth
But came to his Calvary.
Jesus had followed the star of his birth.
Well I remember, said old Zebedee.

After a whiley the laddies came back
With Peter and Andrew and others.
I was right glad to see them and hear all their crack,
The ifs and the ans, and the to's and the t'others.
A wonderful story they all had to tell;
Jesus, they said was not dead.
Jesus had told them before his farewell
To haste back to Galilee. That's what he'd said.
So they waited; and day followed yesterday;
They waited by Galilee.
At first with excitement, and then with dismay.
Well I remember, said old Zebedee.

One day says I, 'Jimmy, see here, you, and John;
There's no good just sitting there wishing.
And day and night sighing and groaning like yon,
It's time you were back at the fishing.
The rest of you come if you're wanting to come,
But you'll come if you're wanting your meat.
There's work for you all and it's time you did some;
And if you don't work, you don't eat.
They girned and they grumbled, but they came down the shore
And we ran the boat down to the sea.
Four of them set themselves down to an oar.
Well I remember, said old Zebedee.

I have fished yon loch for a long long while,
But never I knew such a night.
It was moving with fish but could we beguile
A minnow to come to the light!
We cast the net and we cast again,
All night without touching a fin;
We cast and drew with might and main,
But never a fish we brought in.
'Bewitched we are, the devil's abroad
On the loch of Galilee,
Pull for the shore for the love of God.'
Well I remember, said old Zebedee.

Never a fish came into our net
To make our hearts rejoice.
Although we knew there were fish to get.
It was then we heard the voice.
We were close inshore you'll bear in mind,
We could see the man that spoke,
Mistily maybe, and hard to find
Behind a wee pillar of smoke.
He had kindled some driftwood from the shore
That burns with a flame that's blue to see.
Says he, 'Have you meat for one mouth more?'
Well I remember, said old Zebedee.

Peter cries put, 'Not a single scale
Though our arms are sore with the casting.
Not even a codling, far less a whale,
You'll go to your bed, friend, fasting.'
The man says, 'Cast on the other side,
Your luck will change if you wish.
Have another shot, my friends, and I'll bide
And mend my bit fire for the fish.'
It had such a cheery, lightsome sough
That with a one, two, three,
We shot the net into the trough.
Well I remember, said old Zebedee.

I could not tell you, friend, if I durst,
The weight of that single cast.
The net was bulging fit to burst;
We could only haul and make fast.
'It is the Lord; the Lord' they cry
And wow, 'twas a joyful clatter,
And Peter, before you could blink an eye
Was head over heels in the water.
'It is the Lord, the Lord,' they roar
Across still Galilee.
And in ten strong pulls we were on the shore.
Well I remember, said old Zebedee.

And the Lord he handed me a dish,
And he said with a glint in his e'e;
Will I not catch men?
Man, you can't catch fish
Without some help from me.
And from that day on I've cast my net
Into all mankind's sea.
With the help of the Lord I'll land one yet.
Well I remember, said old Zebedee.

Dear God, The Difference

I had met Amos in the hills above Greenock, and he had done most of the talking for he was a better hillman than I was, and had more breath for the job. Jeremiah I had known by the sadness of his voice, and Nehemiah by his expertise as a butler. Isaiah had come to study my books, and Samson to examine my physical condition. Isaiah was more satisfied than Samson was.

But sooner or later this series had to end. It had gone on for fifteen years and more. Not that there was any shortage of material. Maybe the reason why I had not brought it to an end was because I knew and had known all the time, that the last sermon had to be the dialogue with the Master himself. And I was dodging the responsibility of it.

I had written and preached the second last one; if you can have a second last without a last. And it had been a conversation with John the Baptist, a favourite character with me, in spite of what Herod's wife and Oscar Wilde had to say about him.

And John had left me with the words, 'After me cometh one.' There was no doubt about who that one was to be; but how would he come?

This is the trouble with having an excellent local newspaper which everyone reads. They look up the church advertisements on a Saturday and expect to see your subject announced. And you have to put your advertisement in on the Thursday. One Thursday I did it. I advertised the series, which was called 'Wise men look at Greenock': and then took the chance. 'The greatest of them all.'

By ten o'clock on the Saturday night I still didn't know where to start or how to start. I had ideas, of course, maybe clever enough ideas; but just gimmicks. They didn't ring true For this talk between Jesus and myself wouldn't come. We weren't in communion. We weren't on the same wavelength. What was I to look for? What was I to listen for?

'After me cometh one.' The Baptist had said it. But how? Stepping down from a stained glass window ruby red and ringed with a halo? Or out from the canvas of an old master sad eyed, pale, and winsome?

Would he come as John of Patmos saw him in the dream, his head and hair as white as wool, his eyes as a flame of fire, his feet like unto brass as if they burned in a furnace, and voice as the sound of many waters?

I did not know what would give me the lead to the vision of the Lord; I waited, but he did not come.

It had been a hard kind of week. Most of my members would have thought it wasn't half as hard as their week, but most of them would have given up my kind of week by about Wednesday: or maybe Thursday. And now it was Saturday night at ten o'clock. The morning sermon and the children's address (which is sometimes harder) were ready. But not the big one. And I began to doze.

Visits and interviews, problems, my own and other people's; calls on folk who'd heard bad news; letters to be written; a funeral, a wedding, a birth, a death. Kirk Session and Board and not much peace to think, except to think about work, and people. The men who were boys when I was a boy, Paisley and Glasgow and the tea gardens of Assam, and dear Greenock itself.

Black men and white men, and yellow and brown; Scots, English, Irish, Welsh, Dutch and Greek, Nepalese and Bengali. I thought of work and play and taxes and unemployment and newspapers, and hospitals and prisons and cemeteries, and sealing wax and sailing ships and cabbages and kings. It was all just as disconnected as that, and then the sermon began to write itself in a series of bright and unmistakable pictures. And when I had set it all down, and drew the curtains to open the window before going to bed, I saw that it wasn't worth my while, for it was bright morning.

A bus queue in blacked out wartime Greenock, and me nearer the end than the beginning of it. A thick drizzle of not unusual rain. Men with shoulders hunched and collars turned up, women with their hair plastered down by the wet. Faint yellow light shining back from the greasy pavement. Every bus but the right one. Shuffling forward like convicts exercising.

What was I going out for anyway? To see half a dozen folk who didn't particularly want to see me, except to complain about the cost of living and the way the war was going, rationing, and the deficiencies of Greenock Morton, and why the church wasn't warmer last Sunday, and could I do anything to get Isa a house.

The right bus at last. Shuffle forward again. Nearly there. The door is shut with the conductress' valedictory, 'Come on get aff.' And the rain gets colder and heavier.

Somebody's to blame. Blame the bus company, blame the Corporation, blame the folk whose journey isn't necessary, blame the Government, blame everything and everybody in sight and out of sight.

A Palestine village in the brown gloaming. Nine or ten men sitting at the side of the road where the houses begin. Tired men, rubbing their feet. One of them on the short parched grass lies on the broad of his back, hands clasped behind his head, eyes shut. A man dead beat. And hungry too. Blue smoke from evening fires is rising from the clachan, and the breeze brings the savour of the cooking pots, and nostrils twitch hopefully.

Two men come bustling out from the huddle of houses indignation bristling all over them. They hurry to the leader and shake him awake. 'Master,' they stutter; they can hardly speak for their wrath. 'Master, listen. They won't take us in. Nobody'll give us a mouthful of meat. Curse them, Master. Call down fire from heaven on them.'

The Master breathes a long sigh, and sniffs the breeze again, leans back on his arms, his head bowed, then pushes himself up and gets stiffly to his feet. Looks at the darkening village where the lights are beginning to twinkle from the windows, tastes the breeze again and wipes his lips with the back of his hand. Smiles and shrugs his shoulders and begins to walk down the dusty road.

'Come on, lads,' he smiles. 'There's another village three miles on.'

God in heaven, I thought. What makes people so different?

A fresh breeze blowing in over the Cumbraes, bright sun in the sky. Fit as a fiddle and life going well. Lots of folk on the road looking fit as fiddles and with life going well with them too. Then far down the road a wheel chair; a nurse. A boy from the East Park Home; very pale, his face pinched and drawn. Poor wee chap.

We come nearer. There's something beating in my head, a strength struggling in me saying, 'Stand in front of that chair', and stop it. Look into that boy's eyes, take his hands in your strong hands, and say to him, 'Get up and walk!'

We come nearer still. We meet. His eyes are wounded and hurt. He smiles, and we pass. I to my home and he to his.

I would have looked so silly standing there shouting 'Get up and walk', and he not able to stir a muscle, and a crowd beginning to gather and to whisper and then to growl, 'Leave the wee fellow alone. What are you trying to do?'

An old man on a dusty straw bed, and a young man who stopped by his side one white day where the crowd pushed and shoved and jostled. Who stopped and saw no one but the man who needed him. Stopped and looked into the hurt eyes and said, 'Get up, lad; pick up your paliasse; and walk.'

And he did.

Dear God in heaven, I thought. What makes people so different?

She stood in the half dark of an entry waiting to meet some man when the pubs scailed. (When this was done on television the producer's side note on the script was: 'Trace some film, God knows there's plenty of them'.)

Her face had been handsome once, but her way of life had left its marks. A woman with no illusions about God or man. Well, maybe she had some illusions about God. But none about man: quite certainly, none about man. Or should that be 'men'?

Embarrassed maybe: but certainly not ashamed. When a decent couple passed, they glanced, then looked away. And the man glanced again until he got a nudge in the ribs from his wife, and you could see their heads coming together as they whispered their comments, and looked away. And the man wanted to have another look, but was scared to try.

In the minds of those who passed by (especially in the minds of the douce, untempted wives) there was no room for any excuse.

This was a sinner. And hers, unfortunately in the eyes of respectable religion, was the only sin. In their hearts nobody wanted to know her story. Some virtuous people might have been inclined to help if they had been perfectly certain that her fall had been due to circumstances, and not to choice.

And so all the douce respectable people felt more respectable still (and so more douce: a wonderful Scottish word!) because they had seen a sinner. So they hurried on to the company they were trysted to keep; and they left her there alone.

The Master was embarrassed, and he did not look up. Anything unclean always hurt him and made his heart sore. But they insisted that he give an answer.

'We found her soliciting. The Law says stone her. What do you say?'

Still he did not look up, and they grinned in their beards. They had him now. He had wriggled out of a few tight spots. He wouldn't wriggle out of this one.

Jesus scratched on the ground. His eyes were still down

'Let him who is absolutely pure in heart throw the first stone.' He said quite conversationally, and then he looked up. And that look was enough. They saw the scorn and they saw the truth. The truth about themselves that no man or woman wants to face.

Jesus went on making patterns in the dust. He knew that they were going away. He knew that they were sliding away, one trying to avoid his neighbour's eye, and succeeding, because his neighbour was trying to avoid his.

When the last of them had gone, he looked up again. He looked at the woman, and a bonnie woman she was.

'Have they all gone?' he asked her, knowing perfectly well that they had – and why they had. 'Is there no one to condem you?'

'No one,' she whispered. And there was a look of true love in her eyes that had not lighted there for many and many a long day.

'Then neither do I,' he smiled. 'Go your ways and sin no more, lassie. It isn't worth it . . .'

Dear God in heaven, I thought. What makes people so different?

She stood bewildered at the crossing: about nine or ten years old she would be. Her skipping rope was trailing behind her. Her hands were blue. It was a cold night and her coat was thin.

It would be her brother who was with her. A sturdy enough laddie. There were holes in his jersey that could have been darned. His wellingtons were worn, and, I would think, were letting in. It was ten at night, and somebody, passing, said 'poor unwanted bairns'.

I saw him growing up, that boy. A dirty house, a slovenly mother with far more weans than she was fit to cope with or even fit to bear. But you know what a man's like on a Friday night!

Never a story and never a song; reared on chips and pieces and cuffs on the side of the head. Hounded to school for fear of being fined. No love from his teacher. Learning to read and write in books smeared with margarine. Nobody would sit beside him because of his smell.

Collecting beer bottles after the match and hawking them round the pubs. Dead end job on the laundry van. Finding easy ways of making the odd half-crown. Tossing for pennies under the railway bridge. Taste of the cheap red wine. Go at a gas meter. Caught and on the record. Approved school. A marked man. The time he went too far. And maybe then, the river. Five minutes in the cold, then no breath left; peace at last.

A crowd of thoroughly respectable people, all very interested, and for the best of reasons, in their souls' salvation. Listening with reverent and affectionate interest to the Master's words. A Father God; love as the be-all; a place of many mansions.

There's a wee boy who can't sit at peace. Maybe it's the quiet. Maybe he needs the bathroom. The disciples put their heads together. The single men have one answer for his trouble; the married men have another. They decide that he'd be better out of the road.

The Master stops his discourse. With his finger he beckons the boy to him, and he comes, thumb in his mouth. Jesus lifts him up to the stretch of his arms, then sits him on his knee and rumples his hair.

'If any man offend against one such little one, it were better that an outsize millstone were hanged about his neck and he was drowned in the deepest depths of the sea.'

Dear God, in heaven, I thought. What makes people so different?

And there were other pictures and there were other words.

I saw the old Modeller (and this is not a man who makes models, but a man who lives in a model lodging house, and I have known many of them), I saw him standing in the gutter, his face well painted by the methylated spirit of his Saturday drinking, standing in the gutter on the Sabbath day as the good and godly (and that is written not cynically) passed by on their way to the kirk. His greasy bunnet outstretched for alms.

And I heard a voice which said: 'A certain man went down from Jerusalem to Jericho . . .'

I saw a man shut the door of his home in the face of a laddie who had shamed him. And I heard a voice which said, 'A certain man had two sons . . .'

I saw an assembly of divines debating the Church's attitude to this and the Church's attitude to that. And I heard a voice which said: 'What is that to thee? Follow thou me.'

I saw a man waver and fail when a tempting and trial of his faith came on him. And I saw a man kneeling in a garden with the wet of his sweat shining on his face under the Passover moon, who said: 'Father, take away this bitter cup . . . still, not my will, but thine be done.''

I heard the clamour of the market and exchange, where the huxters call and the clever lie in wait for the foolish and ambitious.

And I heard a voice which said two words: 'Thou fool.'

Only voices I heard and pictures of the mind and recollection I saw, before the light of vision died with the light of the morning. But there was one left.

I saw the hill that rises steeply behind my town. A sweep of climbing road, a little park, paths and seats, and a clump of trees. And it was very cold and lonely in the falling winter's night.

Against the greyness of the grey sea and against the straggling lights below, there was the loom of a man who sat, elbows resting on his knees, his face half hidden in his hands.

The marching lamps below showed the street where people live. Picture houses and Bingo Halls, Churches and Chapels, and a hundred thousand immortal souls: a million human hopes and fears.

All wanting something, all hoping for something, and some even praying for something.

Maybe not very clear about what the something is, but wanting it just the same.

And the grey man said, as he sat, chin in hand, looking down over it all. He said: 'Jerusalem, Jerusalem how often? But ye would not.'

Dear God in heaven, I thought, make us, for our own sakes, different.

THE DEVIL IT IS

I was laying a piece of linoleum at the time: a job which is sore on the knees and the temper: I had straightened to ease one of these situations. That was when the voice said:

'Aye, so they say, but it isn't true.' But I hadn't said anything, neither had any 'they' that I could think on. It must have been something I was thinking. What was I thinking anyway?

I'd been thinking about my back. I'd been thinking about linoleum, and not in any respectful language either. What do they say about linoleum: or Kirkcaldy where the linoleum comes from?

'Some say the deil's deid, and buried in Kirkcaldy.'

'Aye, so they say.' It was that same voice again. 'But it isn't true, you know.'

I looked round but there was no one there but the dog. I asked Jasper if he had seen anybody, almost expecting him to say, 'No'. He didn't say anything, he just barked, but not in his usual confident and aggressive way. It was a nervous bark. His eyes were fixed on the door, which was shut. Along his back the hair was beginning to bristle.

I opened the door, Jasper went through it and down the stairs like a scalded cat. Behind me there was a chuckle, a deep well-pleased-with-itself chuckle.

'Invisible, friend,' said the voice, 'but very much alive.'

'Then you must be . . .' I gasped . . .

'Don't bother about names, my friend. I have many names: Satan, Mephistopheles (I rather fancy myself in red tights), Le diable, El diabolo: you Scots show less respect but you're more friendly, with Auld Clootie and Old Nick. I really don't mind; I answer to all of them.'

'But you don't exist!' I tried to sound more convincing than I felt.

'So you're just talking to yourself?' He chuckled.

'Yes, of course, that's what it is. I'm just talking to myself.' I was ready to grasp at any straw.

'Then you must be a right devil.' The laugh was the kind that used to terrify Faust. It shook me. But there isn't any real devil, I told myself. Nobody's ever seen a real devil. I said so.

'A lot of people think they have.' He said 'Forty million Christians can't be wrong.'

'Come out of the shadow, then, and let me have a good look at you.' I was beginning to get more angry than scared.

'Sorry,' he said. 'You can't have a good look at a devil. You can have a bad look, but not a good look.'

'Then let me have a bad look.' I was nearly shouting now.

'You're having one. A bad look never sees anything.'

'But what do you look like?' I did shout this time.

'Why do you want to know?' If ever there was a voice that could grin, that was it.

'So that I'll know you the next time,' I said.

'O, so you think there will be a next time?' He was laughing now. 'You're coming on friend, and fast.'

'But why do you come to see me?' This had been puzzling me from the beginning. 'Professionally I'm one of your trained opposition, you know.'

'Not making much of a job of it though.' He sounded almost sympathetic. I didn't say anything. I didn't want to admit that he was right.

'You may not believe this, friend,' he went on, 'but I really do want to help you. Give you a few hints and that sort of thing. Now don't think I'm flattering you, but I've been watching you for sixty years and I'm forced to the conclusion that you're not at all a bad chap.'

'Thanks very much,' I said, and I must admit that I did feel sightly pleased with myself. 'But why come to see even a reasonably good chap.'

'Not much point in coming to see unreasonably bad chaps at this time of day is there?' It was rather obvious when I thought about it.

'But look,' I persisted, 'even if you really do exist you're something out of the past. You were one of the arch-agels who rebelled against God and you got chucked out of heaven. 'Or do you want me to quote from Paradise Lost?'

'No need,' he said affably. As a matter of fact I gave John Milton a hand to write it. I got so many good bad ideas over with John's help that you'd never believe it.'

'Just you cling to your old ideas, my friend, it suits me very well. Give me horns and a tail, clap me in tights and give me bass solos to sing. That's the way I like people to think of me.'

'Why?' I asked.

'For obvious reasons.' He seemed surprised that I had not understood. 'If they think of me for what I'm not, then they can't think of me for what I am. It's as simple as that.'

'And what are you?" I was getting desperate.

'Well, sometimes I'm this and sometimes I'm that: but old-fashioned is something I never am.'

'As an idea you're old-fashioned.' I grunted.

'Old, yes,' he conceded judicially. 'Old-fashioned, most definitely no. Take stars for example.'

'Very well then,' said I, 'let's take stars. What kind of stars?'

'Stars in the newspapers,' he explained as to a little child 'Nobody could sell a popular newspaper nowadays without a horoscope column, could they? Of course you'll never look at it?' It wasn't so much a statement as a question. I did answer it. I have a conscience.

'Not seriously of course,' I excused myself without much conviction. But he agreed with me. An intelligent chap like myself would never take a thing like that seriously. I felt I could quite get to like this fellow in time. He was so understanding.

'But why do people do this nowadays?' I asked. 'We living in the most scientific age the world has ever known. Why consult horoscopes?'

'Just for the same reason that they did it 5000, or 2000 years ago. They're scared.' I asked what they were scared about.

'Anything that people don't understand they fear: and your world simply doesn't understand anything. O they can explain things, but they can't explain anything that matters. They can give the "how" of this, that, and the next thing, but they can't give the "why" of anything. So they're scared.'

'Just ignorant folk,' I protested. He laughed heartily and long.

'Not on your life, friend, not on your sweet life. Ignorant folk don't look for anything, and they certainly don't look forward. Today's good enough or bad enough for them. It's not the ignorant, it's the clever folk, who don't appreciate that cleverness is not wisdom. It took me years of work to get cleverness and wisdom confused, but you must agree that I've made a pretty good job of it.' I had to agree, but I didn't say so.

'The big struggle was to get people to believe in evolution, he went on. 'And I must admit that your church put up a pretty stout fight against it. But of course I was at work there too.'

'At work in the church!' I gasped.

'Of course,' he chuckled. 'One of my most profitable lines. On the evolution business the church could have damaged me if they had taken up a commonsense position. Science and religion might have started to work together. But the church very nearly proved to its own satisfaction that the world was flat; and so the great cleavage came. Another mark chalked up for me; and since then the two have grown further and further apart till they just don't speak the same language any more, and people have got an idea of evolution that refuses to see religion anywhere. Every day and in every way the world's getting better and better. If you've enough patience and time you'll see the millennium. But they're not so sure now. It isn't coming quick enough; and they've got nothing else, and isn't good enough. So they're scared, and they're searching the stars. They always have done.'

'And always will?' I asked doubtfully.

'I see no reason at all why they should not.' He had no doubt at all. 'They're logical people, but logic doesn't produce answers; they're reasonable people, but reason creates only more questions. Goodness gracious – or rather badness ungracious – you talk of progress and the evolution of humanity! Twenty-five years ago civilized people were doing things to one another that would have put my old friend Attila the Hun and the Emperor Nero off their sleep. And they're still doing it in this year of disgrace.'

'Then surely what you're saying,' I said quietly, 'is that the only hope is religion?'

'Of course that's what I'm saying,' the voice almost suggested that he would have been immortally offended if I had said anything else.

'This is where I want to help you. I know it may appear odd to you, but look at it from my point of view. If they go on as they're going they won't believe in anything.'

'You mean that if they stop believing in God they stop believing in you?' I could see the point. Unless you know what is good you can't possible know what is bad.

'Of course that's what I mean,' he went on persuasively. 'But you're losing your grip: you've got to get it again.'

'How would you suggest?' Mind you I was a bit wary, but I wanted to know just the same.

'Get rid of the things that modern man can't swallow. Get rid of the stumbling blocks – that's what Paul called them wasn't it?' I just nodded: this chap was prepared to take on Paul too.

'For one thing there's the Bible. Now I admit that the Bible is full of truth, but it's old fashioned, much of it is irrelevant. It doesn't speak to people any more. You're intelligent people living in the twentieth century. Nobody should be asked to believe in anything that can't be proved. You've got to broaden your ideas; come and go a bit more with those who ask questions.'

'You mean come and go on the answers.' I was beginning to get the drift of things now.

'Always according to conscience,' he said, and there was a genuine ring of piety in his voice, though I couldn't believe it was a ring of genuine piety. 'But you see, your conscience can be conditioned by wrong ideas, and if it is, then it must obviously be an imperfect conscience. Don't think for a moment, my dear chap that I'm going to persuade you to give up your faith or abandon your religion. Nothing could be further from my thoughts. It's your prejudices you've got to give up; not your convictions.'

'Is there all that much difference between a prejudice and a conviction?' I asked him a little uncertainly.

'O, a vast difference.' I had a feeling that he had a feeling that he was beginning to get me on the run: and maybe he wasn't all that far wrong.

'A conviction becomes a prejudice when you stop thinking about it. But a real conviction has got to be examined carefully and continuously in the light of new ideas, and fresh evidence and changing thought, and increasing experience. Look at your vows of church membership for example. Look, if you like, at your own vows of ordination. Would it be an impertinence if I asked when you last read the Westminster Confession of Faith?'

'It wouldn't be an impertinence.' I was a little embarrassed 'It would be an impossibility.'

'There you are then.' He must have been expecting that answer. 'And that's only one example. Think it over.'

'I might,' I said doubtfully. As a matter of fact I was already thinking it over.

'Fear is the trouble,' he went on soothingly. 'And fear comes out of ignorance. It's failure to face the facts of life that cause fear. You can't explain anything that's happening in the world if you apply the old answers and the old truths – truth within quotation marks, I hasten to add. You've got to again.'

'But you've already said' (I thought I had him here), 'that it's thinking people who're more scared than anyone That must be because they are thinking instead of accepting.'

'Not at all,' he corrected me in a kindly way. 'It's because they are not thinking far enough. They haven't found their own explanation and they can't accept yours. You've go to get together. You've both got to compromise: the alleged Christian and the avowed agnostic.'

I wondered whom an agnostic is supposed to avow himself to, but I didn't mention it.

'There you are,' he went on, 'a reasonably intelligent chap: who's been preaching the gospel for – how long?'

'More than forty years, man and boy,' I admitted.

'More than forty years. At home and abroad, in town and country, and broadcasting too, speaking to millions and millions of people, and you're not all that sure of things yourself. You don't believe any more than I do that the world and it's people inevitably and steadily grow better. More and more you're being driven back to the idea that there's some baneful force at work in the world knocking things down as soon as they are built up, dragging things back as soon as they look like improving.'

'And is there?' I asked. He laughed loud and long.

'What do you think?' he choked.

'You devil!' I said to myself. Half and hour ago I would have said it was impossible, unthinkable, that in the world there should be an evil force working against God and good I would have said that the world couldn't possibly be a battle ground between God and the devil with the souls of men as the winner's prize. God cannot be defeated and still be God. Why should I feel uncertain now? Why has good become bad a bad become good? Could people still sell their souls to the devil? Is there a spirit that comes raging up from the gloom and fire of hell to destroy the best that has been made by the white spirit of heaven?'

'I'm waiting for an answer,' said the voice, 'though there's no immediate hurry. I have all the time in the world.' And I had no answer. What is evil? Who made evil?

'Who made you?' I blurted out, 'If you are anything that was made? You couldn't create yourself could you?'

'You'd be surprised at what I can do,' he chortled.

'No,' I said. 'I'm not surprised at what you can do; I'm just surprised that you are allowed to do it.'

'And who's to stop me?' He was quite indignant.

'God, surely.' I hoped I sounded more confident than I felt. He sneered.

'God? How should God be able to make me do what I don't want to do when God can't even make you do what you don't want to do? Admit it now, God can't force you to do anything. Does that make Him omnipotent? If God can create a man who can oppose him, why can't he create a devil who can oppose him? Or are we created at all?'

'But . . .' I began and got no further.

'God's creation,' and the contempt in his voice! 'Dachau and Belsen; Nagasaki and Hiroshima; Vietnam and Biafra; apartheid; keep Britain white; heads down for bingo; God's servants carrying out God's purpose? Who are you kidding friend? Me or yourself?'

I scratched my head with the tacklifter. The chuckles we coming fast and furious from the corner. Then they stopped as if a tap had been turned off. A voice said:

'So this is where you are, Lucifer.' There was something about that voice that made me feel he was Lucifer's match, though I was in no punning mood.

'Well, well, well,' said Lucifer, but the old jauntiness was missing. 'If it isn't old Michael himself. How are you my dear ex-colleague, and Gabriel and the other archangels?'

'Well enough,' said Michael. 'Kept rather busy these days, as I see you are yourself.'

'Yes,' said Lucifer with a pretended weariness. 'The daily round, the common task that brings its own reward. I've just been having a most interesting conversation with our clerical friend, here. You know, Michael, he can't see me.'

'Dear me,' said Michael. 'I wonder if he can see me?' But I couldn't. I looked very hard, but I had to admit that I couldn't.

'Not so good,' said Michael sadly, and I'm sure he was shaking his head reprovingly. 'You're in a bad way, friend. But there's nothing unusual about it. Very few people see angels nowadays.'

'Except half-wits,' Lucifer sniggered.

'And children,' Michael said gently. Lucifer did not comment. I was feeling my position very keenly. Here was in the presence of good and evil and I couldn't tell the difference.

'Tell me Michael,' I said nervously when the silence had become unbearable, 'tell me how to see you and where to find you who are the power of good and the spirit of man, where am I to look for you . . . please?

'Look for me in history, my friend,' and his voice was very kind and understanding. 'You'll find Lucifer there too, of course. In fact if you find him you'll always find me.'

'Where in history?' I said.

'Anywhere,' he answered. 'What were you talking about when I came in?'

'Fear,' I said. 'Fear and superstition, and cleverness, and power, and cruelty, and the stars.'

'Then if you know anything about history, go back some nineteen hundred years.' And I sent my mind searching back.

The great Roman Empire that even then was beginning to crumble and to totter to its fall; the mystery religions flourishing with their strange rites and initiations, and their searching of the stars. And down in the catacombs beneath the eternal city the slaves, the oppressed, the exiles, gathering by the little Christian sign of the fish and singing the first Christian hymn:

> He hath put down the mighty from their seats,
> And exalted them of low degree;
> He hath filled the hungry with good things
> And the rich he hath sent empty away.

I spoke the great words of Mary's hymn quietly, and asked Michael if this is what he meant.

'Yes,' he said approvingly, 'that is what I meant. You thought you had it all your own way then, didn't you, Lucifer?'

From the corner there came a disgruntled grunt.

'Yes, Lucifer' Michael went on, 'you had them all looking for their stars and running away to hide from what they saw there: trying to get away from the baneful force that held them in thrall, and you thought there was no place for them to go.

'I was winning.' Lucifer was defiant. Then he sighed. 'I had them all running away from reality, and then that hideous swarm of yours came crawling up from the catacombs, and the whole world cracked.'

'But I'm not done yet, Michael,' he said grimly. 'O I know you've won every round so far, but all the time it has been a close run thing. Don't think you'll get away with it all the time. They're coming round to my ways again and they're coming fast. I've got the world split down the middle and I've got plenty of friends on both sides in places high and places low. And I've got the moon, and I've got space, but more than all I've got time. And now, if you will excuse me, I have more important things to do than argue with a sixty-year-old parson who's telling other people where to stand when he doesn't know where he stands himself. We will all meet again I have no doubt.'

'I have no doubt either, Lucifer; and if it is any comfort to our friend I will assure him here and now that he will never meet you without meeting me as well.'

Lucifer said no more, but the room seemed to grow lighter and I knew that he was gone. I cleared my throat nervously

'Michael,' I whispered, 'are you still here?'

'Yes,' he said quietly, 'I am still here.'

'Michael,' I went on, 'I hate to admit this; but I'm still scared.'

'So you ought to be,' said Michael grimly, 'so should everybody be. It depends what you're scared of. What are you scared of? Is it Lucifer?'

'No, not exactly Lucifer.' I found this hard to explain. 'More what he stands for. I won't say that he's winning, but he seems to be keeping you from winning; keeping God from winning. And that's as bad, isn't it? The world always seems to be getting somewhere and then something happens and we're back where we started. It's like the snakes and ladders we played when we were kids; you climb so slowly up the ladders and you're just within sight of the top when there's the snake and you go sliding down again. When will God's way begin to work, Michael?'

'It's rather hard to explain,' and Michael's voice was very kind. 'You talk about "when" and with God there is no when. It is always "now". The victory is won; evil has been conquered. But you all keep creating it again. You must make up your minds that evil is nothing; and that only God is real. Only love is real. Everything else is false. Think for a moment of evils that men have created and ask where they are now.' And so I did.

The ancient world secure on the shoulders of its slaves; and the Cross comes, and it goes down to dust. It was all a sham with no substance in it at all; and a sham cannot face the truth. 'Ye shall know the truth and the truth shall make ye free.'

The church itself and what it became; half a world stumbling through a man-made darkness. Then a voice, and the light breaks through. 'Ye shall know the truth and the truth shall make ye free.'

The Bastille frowning over frightened France, a hand stretches strongly out and the grim doors creak open and one tyranny dies. 'Ye shall know the truth and the truth shall make ye free.'

The pits, exploitation of humanity, the mills, the potteries, the climbing boys: a handful of men, and it goes down to death. 'Ye shall know the truth, and the truth shall make ye free.'

Mussolini, Hitler, Stalin, where are they now? And I saw what Michael meant and I said that I saw, but there was no word from him, and I knew that I was alone and had been alone all the time, and that what I had believed in my heart was not a silly optimism, but that it was the truth that had been from the beginning of time.

That good must always defeat evil if good is pursued with a passion equal to that of those who pursue evil. That truth defeats falsehood when the passion for it is equal. That it is the passion that matters.

The door was pushed open and I gave a jump; but it was only Jasper, carrying his tail a little low, I thought. He sniffed around the room, paying particular attention to the corner from which Lucifer's voice had come. But Jasper seemed satisfied: there was no smell of brimstone, but just of linoleum.

So I turned back to the job in hand and got down on my knees; which is not a bad position at the start or finish of any enterprise.

COCK CROW

THIS is the story that Peter once told:
Simon called Peter, ye mind o' the name.
The tale of the night of the bitterest cold,
And of Simon called Peter, his bitterest shame.

Peter was old when he told this tale,
Old he was, weary, and bowed wi' the years.
His sight and his hearing had started to fail,
And Simon was haunted by terrible fears
That when Peter was dead and happed in his grave
(And each year it grew closer, as old Simon kenned)
The last of the Twelve would have then joined the lave,
And never a word of the good Master's penned.
Never a word written down in ink
Of the life and the death of the Lord!
And he was the last of them, Peter would think,
That had heard Jesus' call; that had sat at the board
In the room with the wine and the bread;
That had sat with the Master in yon upper room.
Who's to tell that tale when Simon is dead?
Of the garden, and cross, and the tomb?
The tale of the triumph, yon day that we ran,
At the Magdalene's bidding to find out it was true?
The rising of Jesus! Set it down while ye can.
There's not a disciple still living, but you.

So he bade John Mark take parchment and pen,
For John and old Simon in these days kept tryst:
'Ye can start and write', said Simon then,
'The beginning of the Gospel of the Lord Jesus Christ.'

So Peter remembered, and John Mark set down
The tale that he had to tell:

Of Galilee lake and Jerusalem town,
And the Upper Room and the Lord's farewell;
And the sun went down, and the stars shone bright –
Just a voice and the scrape of a pen –
As John set down by the candlelight
The tale of the Lord and His men.
Till they came to the night of the Upper Room,
And the supper that was the last,
And the Paschal moon and Gethsemane's gloom
And Judas, forever outcast.
Peter stopped, and Mark said 'What's ado?'
Laid down his pen and came to his side.
'Simon we've worked the whole night through,
The rest of the story can bide.'
He took in his own hand the old withered hand,
'Let me help you, old friend, to your rest.'
'We'll go on,' said old Simon; 'You must understand
That the worst's to go down with the best.'

'Up till now it's the glory, the pride and the place
Of the Rock –'twas the Master's own name.
You've writ of my greatness, you've writ of my grace,
Now you'll write of my sorrow and shame.'

Mark smiled at old Peter, and then he went down
And knelt by the side of his chair;
With a tear in his eye, Peter stared at the ground.
'Peter,' said Mark, 'I was there.'
John reached forward his hand, and there in the palm
Was the scar from the slash of the sword;
'Remember old friend the lad that I am,
I was there when they prisoned the Lord.
I was there when they nailed him to Calvary's tree;
I was there with the rest on the hill;
This is John Mark, Simon: Peter, it's me,
We knelt there together until
He cried "It is finished", and Jesus was dead,
Your story and mine now are one.
Come away, Simon, it's time for your bed,

I'll not lay pen down till I'm done.'
'In my mother's house, where we'd hidden before,
We hid for the fear of the Jews.
I was the laddie who opened the door,
When Mary brought to us the news.'

'So you know it all?' Simon said with a smile,
And he patted Mark's hand on his knee:
'So there's nothing I've carried this long and long while,
Known by none but the Master and Me?'
I've never confessed it; I've bided my time;
But I think that the time now is run,
For Simon's confession; for Peter's downclimb;
We'll finish what we have begun.

'The Master forgave me it, lang, and lang syne,
His way's not to cast up your sin;
But this is His Gospel: not yours and not mine,
So my secret has got to go in.
Then sit you down, Johnnie, and pick up your pen,
And dip it again in the ink.
It'll help you a wee in your judgment of men
If you learn that I'm not all you think.

'When Judas came there with the priest and his pack
And the lot of us took to our heels;
I waited a wee on the hill, then came back,
Treading soft as the jackal steals.
They took the good Lord to the house of the priest,
And they hurried him into the hall;
You'll mind 'twas the night of the Passover feast,
And the moonlight was white on the wall.

'It was cold, bitter cold, in the High Priest's court,
And the Passover moon shone white;
They took the good Lord for their Passover sport,
To liven their Passover night.
They laughed and they skirled, they sang and they cheered,
They argued and quarrelled and fought;

They crowded the windows, they poked and they peered
To see him whose life the priest sought.
Now and again one would come to the door,
To tell them what happened within;
They would listen a while, and then they would roar
For the price of the Nazarene's sin.

'So the night drove on till the moon hung low,
And the mob 'gan to tire of their play.
The night was too cold and the sport was too slow,
So they yawned, and they shouldered away.

'But not very far from me, near to the stair,
Some callan had kindled some coals;
A score of the priestly had gathered round there,
Warming their bodies and souls.
They were cooried around with their hands to the blaze,
And their shadows were black on the wall.
The blue of the smoke hung above in a haze
And they spoke of the man in the hall.

'I heard the name, Jesus: I thought, here's a friend!
I'll go closer and hear what he'll say.
Maybe there's more; we can win in the end;
We can rescue the Lord and away.
The thought had come to me, to tell you the truth,
It might be the Lord's men, Andrew, the brothers!
If they'd come back too, then by God and forsooth!
But it wasn't his friends. It was others.

'I stood at the edge of them, there in the dark,
And looked at them there in the red.
But of pity or mercy there was not a spark;
They wanted the Nazarene dead.

Says I to myself then, it's time you were gone,
There's no one but enemies here;
You're all by yourself, and there's naught to be done;
And boldness could cost you too dear.

'It was then that a lassie came out through the door,
With a pitcher to fill at the well.
And one of them shouts to her, "Wench, how long more
Will they need there to send him to hell?"

'She came over to join in the crack and the chaff;
She was quick in the tongue, yon, and smart.
And she turned round to me with a wink and a laugh,
And says, "Why, my man, stand ye apart?
Come in with the rest of us here and get warm,
Let's look at you nearer the light;
Are you feared that a lassie could do you some harm?
We've had trouble enough for the night."

'I shrugged her away, and I brushed down her hand
That was holding the slack of my sleeve.
She says, "You should learn better manners, my man."
Says I, "I'll go past, by your leave."

'No sooner I'd said it, I knew my mistake;
For they were all townsfolk, you see.
We've a tongue of our own, we that live by the lake:
There's an accent that's Galilee.
She was on it at once, my Galilee speech.
She cried, "Now I know where you've been!
You're one of the twelve that the man used to teach;
You're a friend of yon Nazarene."

'Then the circle fell silent; as silent as death.
They turned every man round to see.
My heart was like lead. With a catch in my breath,
I whispered, "No' me friends; no' me.
Let me go, mistress, please, let me go on my way;

I have nothing to do with this man.
See, the lift's growing light, and it soon will be day,
I must travel as far as I can.
See, the moon is near set; see the rose in the west,
Twill be dawn in an hour or so."

And then, like a sword driven through my breast,
I heard the first cock crow.

'That's when I remembered the word of the Lord
When I'd said I would follow till death
A word I'd forgot, but that I should have stored
In my soul till my very last breath.

'The maid said no more, but she stood for a space,
Then she turned to go to the well.
"Leave him alone, lads, just look at his face!
There's a man on the hot hobs of hell.
Though you and me know that the cratur has lied,
I'll tell you the judgement to give:
Let him live when the Nazarene's crucified.
Let him live and be damned! Let him live!"

Now you'll write it all down, John, the way that I've said;
You'll write it all down in your book;
The braggart disciple that made himself head,
And the terrible way that he took.
That's the story that's known to the Master and me,
And now, John, you know it as well.
Write it down for the faithful of all time to see;
Write it down to be read when the bell
Calls the church to the worship of Jesus the King;
And the bairnies are taught in the school.
Write the story of me and the terrible thing
That made Jesus' bitter cup full.

So John Mark wrote it down, the tale he was told,
And sadly he wrote it and slow.
Of Peter the leader, of Peter the bold,
And the night that he heard the cock crow.

When he finished, he turned, and he smiled to his friend.
'But you proved yourself, Peter, the Rock.
And the lesson that's here for mankind to the end,
Is, the last word's not left to the cock.'

Two Men, One Problem

THERE had been a sermon on 'The Word' in a Teaching Mission which the Presbytery organised once in Greenock. And the Word is the authority for preaching and for listening.

There had been a sermon on God the Creator, and the rebellion of men who thought themselves to be as God. Next Sunday's sermon was to be on the mercy of God. For sovereignty without mercy is tyranny; and God is no tyrant. Off and on through the week I was thinking of just how to approach the subject, and not getting very far with the thinking.

Which example, which illustration, what line of thought? There was the mercy of the Psalms; especially maybe, of the hundred and third: 'The Lord is merciful and gracious, slow to anger; plenteous in mercy.'

And of course the great and everlasting mercy of God, who proved on Calvary that God is love and love is God, and so neither can die. There was the mercy of the prophet who said that God would never utterly destroy, and, of course the mercy of the great parable of forgiveness.

The day had been hard, the fire was warm, and as I often do, I fell into a dwam, which may be translated as a trance.

And then there were two men sitting on the couch at the other side of the fire. One was older than the other, but he was not very old either. He said:

'Good evening to you. Correct me if I am wrong, but I think you were wondering how you would talk to your people on Sunday about the mercy of God.' I said he was perfectly right. That was what I had been thinking about.

'We've been sent to help you. I think you know me, for we have met before.'

I knew I had seen him before somewhere and it didn't take me long to place him.

'Of course,' I said. 'You are Hosea.' He bowed.

'May I present my friend who does not have a name. This is the Prodigal Son.'

'But,' I gasped, 'there isn't any Prodigal Son. He's just a character in a story.'

'O no he's not.' The Prodigal smiled, a very charming and boyish smile. 'No he's not just a character out of a story. I'm real because I've been made real. Folk have thought about me and read about me and talked about me and preached about me so long and so often, that I have become a person. I'm all the people who ever did what Jesus said I did. And I have come out of the Word with my old friend Hosea, to help you speak of the mercy of God to your people on Sunday.'

'Thank you very much,' said I gratefully. 'I could certainly do with some help. The subject's too big. I don't know where to start.'

'It's where you finish that matters most,' Hosea smiled. 'But you would have some idea for a beginning?'

'Yes,' I nodded. 'There was a quotation from Shakespeare buzzing around in my head.'

'What quotation would that be, I wonder?' said the Prodigal, and added that Hosea and he knew Shakespeare very well.

'I know the one it will be,' said Hosea and began to recite:

> *'The quality of mercy is not strained,*
> *It droppeth as the gentle rain from heaven*
> *Upon the place beneath; it is twice blessed,*
> *It blesseth him that gives and him that takes.*
> *'Tis mightiest in the mightiest; it becomes*
> *The thronèd monarch better than his crown.*
> *His sceptre shows the force of temporal power,*
> *The attribute of awe and majesty,*
> *Wherein doth sit the dread and fear of kings.*
> *But mercy is above this sceptred sway;*
> *It is enthronèd in the heart of kings;*
> *It is an attribute to God Himself,*
> *And earthly power doth then show likest God's*
> *When mercy seasons justice . . .*
> *That in the course of justice none of us*
> *Should see salvation; we do pray for mercy;*
> *And that same prayer doth teach us all*
> *To render the deeds of mercy.'*

'Was that the one?'

'I'll guarantee it was,' the Prodigal smiled. I nodded, and asked if I would have been right to use it.

'Absolutely,' said Hosea.

'Certainly,' said the Prodigal. 'They're true to the last letter. I should know.'

'So should I,' said Hosea. 'It blesseth him that gives and him that takes. You agree, Prodigal?'

'All the way and beyond, Hosea. I was a taker and I was blessed.'

'I was a giver, and I was blessed,' said Hosea.

'Then you two are the proof of it. Taker and giver, and both blessed?'

'More than you know, brother,' said Hosea, and the Prodigal nodded and smiled, and said, 'Yes, brother, more than you know.'

I didn't say anything, for I could see by their faces that their thoughts were far away, and that they would speak in their own good time when their thoughts came back to them. Then the Prodigal sighed.

'Ah yes,' he said. 'What a wonderful thing it is to look for justice and to find mercy.'

'Did you come home looking for justice?' I asked a little timidly.

'Not exactly,' he chuckled.' I came home looking for food.,

'Then you weren't sorry?' I was somewhat shocked I will admit.

'Not terribly sorry.' He leaned back and clasped his hands behind his head. 'O yes, I was sorry I had made a fool of myself, but even sorrier that I had to admit it. I was sorry I'd had to come home with my tail between my legs, but I wasn't sorry I'd gone to the far country.' That shook me more than somewhat.

'But I always reckoned that the far country is a place to be avoided like the plague.'

'Not at all.' The Prodigal took his eyes off the ceiling and looked at me and smiled. 'No, no, nothing of the kind. There's nothing wrong with the far country: it's the wasting your substance in riotous living that's the daft thing to do. If I had behaved myself I could have come back proudly to my father, and said, "Father, I have succeeded, and now I'm really worthy to be called your son".'

'And what would your father have said to that?' I asked.

Hosea laughed. 'He would probably have said "Well done, good and faithful servant".' The Prodigal joined the laugh.

I thought it over for a moment, then said, 'Just to get things straight. You mean there's nothing wrong in going to the far country, so long as you conduct yourself in such a way that you come home with honour?'

'That's right,' said the Prodigal. 'Don't forget whose son you are, and don't forget who gave you your portion of goods.'

'And you forgot?' I asked, rather unnecessarily maybe.

'No. I just never tried to remember. So I remembered when it was too late, and came home.'

'Why?' I asked.

'Because there was no place else to go.'

'I see the point,' I agreed. 'There was no place else to go, so you came home. Looking for what?'

'Food, clothes, shelter,' he grinned, 'but the greatest of these was food.'

'But surely you didn't expect to get them?'

'O yes, I expected to get them.' He was serious now. 'But at a price.' I asked him what price.

'The price that justice demanded. To be made one of his hired servants, who, you will remember had bread enough and to spare.'

'Now look, friend.' I hoped I didn't sound as cynical as I felt. 'You didn't really and honestly expect to pay that price. You knew your father a lot better than that. No, friend,' he said, and stretched out his arms. 'I didn't know my father at all, for all the years I'd lived with him. I didn't know him at all till I came home. I'd thought my father was just an older edition of my brother. I found that he wasn't.'

'Then can we get back to the price?' I asked. There was no arguing about the other matter of relationship.

'Yes, the price.' He clasped his hands between his knees. 'I was ready to pay the price and there was no price. A ring on my finger: no price. Shoes on my feet: no price. The best robe: no price. These things, you see, Jimmy, are beyond price. These are the things that money can't buy. These are the things that only love can give.'

And I thought to myself, how right you are, friend! What shall I render unto the Lord for all His goodness unto me? I will take the cup of salvation. The Prodigal is right, so right; there is no price, there is nothing to pay, the only thanks love wants for loving is that you should take more of it.

'What happened then?' I asked.

'What happened then?' he echoed. 'I woke up.'

'Then . . . then . . . it was all a dream?' I stammered.

'No, no,' he laughed. 'I mean I woke up the next morning.'

'And found the whole world changed, so you lived happily ever after.' I saw the point. He shook his head.

'That's how fairy tales end. This was no fairy tale; this was real. I found that nothing had changed, except myself. And so I lived happily ever after. I saw the old world with new eyes, and I didn't want the far country any more. And so in the end I paid the only price my father wanted. The only price my father would ever have accepted: I gave him back the love that he had given to me. I sought justice; I found mercy. I went home looking for a parent; and I found my father.'

He leaned back again and put his hands behind his head, like a man well content with life; and Hosea who had been lying back, saying very little, sat up and took over.

'That's one side of it,' he said. 'And now you can sit back, and let me show Jimmy the other side of the coin.' I sat up, too, and said: 'Which is?'

'Which is that there are two ways to find out that God is merciful,' said Hosea. 'One is the way of our young friend, here: come admitting that you have made a mess of things, and asking for another chance, which you always get, on any conditions that God may impose, and then finding that you get the other chance without any conditions at all. The other way is the way I found.'

I didn't interrupt or ask silly questions. By the look on his face, Hosea was ready to go ahead. He was just arranging his thoughts. I was right. So he was.

'Tell your people about me on Sunday,' he said reminiscently. 'Tell them I was one of those morose and gloomy souls who think that the whole world's out of step but themselves. You know the type; you must have met them dozens of times.'

I had, but I still didn't interrupt.

'Too thoughtful in one way of thinking, maybe. But there's so many folk who just don't think at all; so there's maybe some excuse for us. We don't get any kick out of life. We develop a sour outlook on things. We tend to sit in judgement. Maybe we're a wee bit jealous of the fun other people get, and that we have been too backward to come forward for. Pleasures to us are a waste of time, maybe because we were frightened we'd be rebuffed if we looked for them. Mainly the pleasures of love. I don't say "sex": just the pleasures of love. We're frightened we won't be loved the way we want to be loved. And we aren't very sure how we want to be loved. So we grudge it to other folk.

'Mind you, we're not as miserable as we're made out to be. We're a whole lot better than those who laugh at us; but I will admit that we're not just the cheeriest of company.

'Getting married was a thing that had never entered my head. No, that's not true. The idea had entered my head, but I didn't know where to start. Fear of the rebuff, again. I didn't go where there were girls to talk to. I wouldn't have known what to talk about. And yet . . .'

He paused for a moment, and something lit up his face as a memory came to him.

'And yet the loveliest girl in all the countryside fell in love with me. As I had fallen in love with her long before, and had done nothing about it. But she did: and we were married.

'It was a runaway marriage, and maybe not the wisest of marriages. Not the kind of marriage a chap like me could have been expected to make. Everybody was surprised when Gomer took me; but nobody was more surprised than I was.

'But there it is, and there's no accounting for it. And these things happen.

'For a while we lived in a little paradise that we made for ourselves, and the first year or two were like a foretaste of heaven. The children came along by and by; two boys and a girl. Our cottage on the hill was heaven on earth. For a while.

'And then things began to go wrong. The neighbours had been wondering when things would go wrong. Not wondering "if"; just wondering "when".

I wasn't earning much money. Nobody seemed to want the work I could do. Others got on. I stuck. I wasn't giving my wife and the kids what I wanted to give them. And you know how it goes.

'To get away from blaming myself, I began to blame them: especially Gomer. I snapped at every word I could twist into a criticism of myself. Instead of skylarking with the bairns before they went to their beds, I would sulk in a corner and tell them to make less noise. Their father had had a hard day's work and deserved some peace and quiet in his own house.

'And then Gomer would tell me I had changed; and I would say the trouble was that she hadn't changed: that she was still as cat-witted as she'd been when I married her. And then the children would begin to cry, and I would bang out of the door girning that a man couldn't be left in peace, and that they were all ganging up against me.

'One night I came home, even wearier than usual. And that means gey weary. I'd been looking for work all day, and getting none. I hadn't tuppence in my pocket.

'The bairns were in bed, but they weren't sleeping. When I asked them why they were bedded down so early, the oldest said he didn't know. He said their mother had told them to get their things off, and then she'd tucked them in, and cried a bit, and kissed them, and gone out. She hadn't said where she was going.

'In the morning I found she'd gone down to the temple, and had become one of the entertainers. At least that's what they called them; entertainers. There's another word for it.

'But now she could have all the trinkets and the trappings that she wanted; but her body belonged to the priests and her soul was sold to the devil.

'I cursed her, and went home.' And Hosea choked when he said the word 'home'.

'A man half mad with jealousy and hate, clutching a grievance close to his cold, sour heart. Seeing the neighbours bobbing their heads as they gossiped; then stopping and waiting till I was by, and starting again, as I knew without seeing them, behind my back. Three motherless bairns, ill-fed, ill-clad. A cold empty hearth, and a cold empty heart.

'I did what I could, and God knows that was little enough. I would lie sleepless, thinking of her down there. I could hear the children whimpering for their mother. And I hated her for what she had done to me; not so much for what she had done to them; but for the shame she had brought to me. What had I done to deserve this last injustice of shame and bitterness?

'I would sit by the ash-grey grate, and I could see her everywhere. Her old housecoat hung on the peg behind the kitchen door, and it spoke to me of her. I could hear her laugh in the song of the burn that passed the door, I could hear her song in the sough of the wind in the trees.

'And then I knew that I needed her. And in that moment, when I admitted to myself that I needed her, I knew that she needed me.'

'In the morning first thing, I went back to the temple. And a big slab-sided, pot-bellied priest laughed at me when I told him my errand.

'It'll cost ye a pretty penny, little man,' says he.

'And what will it cost?' says I, though the hate of him was raging inside of me.

'It'll cost ye fifteen pieces of silver and a homer and a half of barley and cheap at the price,' says he, and he laughed again till his belly rumbled.

'And I sold all that I had, and day and night I worked; and the neighbours were good and they gave me work, for they knew what I was working for. Everything I sold but the cottage on the hill by the side of the burn. And I bought her back. And glad she was to be back with the children and with me.'

He said no more, but sat in silence with a strange sad smile on his face. And the Prodigal reached out his hand, covered Hosea's hand and pressed it, where it rested on his knee. I cleared my throat. Some comment was surely expected from me.

'One thing, Hosea,' I said diffidently. 'I hardly know how to put this for fear of hurting you. But weren't things different between you after that?'

'Of course they were different,' he said. 'But just what are you trying to be at?'

'I just mean,' I said, getting more mixed up than ever through not wanting to say the obvious in an obvious way, 'there was this barrier . . .' His eyebrows went up. I staggered on . . . 'This barrier of the misconduct, of the evil, of the sin. There was a barrier wasn't there?'

'No,' said Hosea. 'There was no barrier. The barrier had been at the beginning. As the years passed, Gomer and I had built that barrier, brick by brick, between us because we both shut our eyes to the one thing that mattered: to the great thing.'

'What great thing?' I whispered.

'This,' said he. 'That I could no more live without her than she could live without me. To discover that great fact, a price had to be paid.'

'But wasn't it too great a price?' I asked, like a fool.

Hosea looked at me, then he looked at the Prodigal. Then they both looked at me and smiled. And maybe there was some pity in that smile.

'For discovering that fact,' said Hosea, 'there is no price too big to pay.' And I was alone again.

And I began to write this sermon: one that was supposed to be on the mercy of God. And I don't know if it is any clearer to you now than it was when you began to read it.

For here is where the two roads meet. The road of giving and the road of taking; and both ways lead to God, whose mercy is given when it is justice you seek; whose nature begins to be known when in your own life you show mercy, and pay the price that mercy demands.

Odd, isn't it, that the one who receives mercy pays nothing? The cost is carried by the one who gives.

God so loved the world that He gave His only begotten Son . . . Who is neighbour unto him that fell among thieves? He that showed mercy and who paid the final two pence.

So, claim the mercy of God according as you show mercy in your life, and qualify for good Martin Elginbrodde's epitaph, which reads:

> *Here lies Martin Elginbrodde;*
> *Have mercy on his soul, O God.*
> *As he would if he was God,*
> *And thou wast Martin Elginbrodde.*

AULD CLAES AND PARRITCH

THE Prodigal son sat up in his bed
And he dichted the sleep frae his e'en.
His heid stounded sair, and his lids were like lead,
And whaur he micht be then, he couldna hae said.
Nor e'en whaur he micht hae been.

Aye his heid was birlin like a mill,
And dry as a bane was his mouth;
Ye ken how it is when ye've had yere fill
O' Auld Kilbaigie, and swats, and yill;
The scunner that follows the drouth.

He yawned and he streetched and he scarted his pow,
And he shivered a wee in the cauld.
Yestreen was the hicht, but the day was the howe;
He was safe hame at laist, like a wanderin' yowe
Come back i' the end tae the fauld.

He glowered at the winnock, and up the camceil
Whaur the paper had peeled frae the wa';
And the raggetty rug whaur a laddie micht kneel
And pray tae be saved frae the wiles o' the deil
And the pride that aye leads til a fa'.

It was no' what ye'd cry a palatial abode,
Yon room at the heid o' the stair;
But for ane that had slep' in a sheuch by the road,
Waur aff nor the nestlins, the brock or the tod,
He couldna hae asked muckle mair.

Hame was never like yon, and it never wad be,
He thocht til himsel as he lay there.
I was owre young and simple yon year I was free,
Gin I'd kent what I ken now, it's there I wad be
And gin ere I win back, man, I'll stay there.

Aye pleesures are like poppies spread,
As weel Burns kenned whan he spak it.
Ye seize the bloom, the flower is shed.
But the Prodigal thocht as he lay in his bed,
That it isna the faut o' the poppy red,
The faut's in the wey that ye tak it.

Had I kenned then what I ken now,
Is the sigh o' the sons o' men.
I wadna debauch and I wadna get fu';
I wad bank a' my siller, and pey a' my due.
But juist in yere lug – there wad be geyan few
Wadna juist dae the same owre again.

Sae the Prodigal thocht as he swung out his leg
And set his fit down on the flair.
I'm ashamed o' my sin, but I'm mair shamed tae beg
Frae them that are gled that I'm taen down a peg.
But gie me hauf a chance and I'll gie them a fleg
Says he, as he cam down the stair.

He'd the ring on his finger, the shune on his feet
And sarkin sae saft on his back.
At the nichtafore pairty his was the tap seat,
And the best o' the wine, and the first o' the meat,
And as muckle o' baith as he'd tak.

They had a' gaithered roun' him, and lauched til they grat,
His haun was still sair wi' the shakin';
Forfochten, disjaskit, bedrailgled and wat,
Wi the dugs barkin daft and auld Baudrons the cat
Rubbin roun his skinned feet as he stood on the mat;
And the faither he aince had forsaken.

But that was last nicht, sirs, and this was the day.
There was wark tae be dune by the feck o' them.
They had nae time tae speak til him, mair nor tae sae
He'd be better in bed yet and out o' their way.
Weel, what mair could a body expect o' them?

He thocht, I'll gae intil the paurlor and sit,
And bide till they cry for the dinner.
I'll juist tak my time, and I'll think for a bit,
On what I'm tae dae gin I'm ever tae fit
And change tae a sanct frae a sinner.

Noo a paurlor's a geyan parteeclar place,
Just for Sawbath's and special occasions;
Wi' its antimacassars and curtains o' lace.
But this auld ferm paurlor had fallen frae grace
On the nicht whan the prodigal first shawed his face
And they roasted the cauf for his rations.

In the cauld licht o' day 'twas sae proud and sae prim
Maist respectable like, and sae douce.
Ye'd neer hae suspected that ocht but a hymn
Had been sung in that paurlor, and never the rim
O' a gless ringed the whatnot sae trig and sae trim;
The verra sanctum o' the hoose.

The walnut piano wi' the lid lockéd, lest
Ye micht fyle the guid ivory keys;
And the fine fretwark front that tae dust was a pest
Whaur in case ye micht pry ower deep in its chest
It wore its reid silk like a modesty vest,
And a scarf that streeched ower its knees.

And the braw overmantel; the black marble clock
And the mug and the braw silver spoon
His grandpa had gied til his big brither Jock;
And chuckies weel polished, and wee bits o' rock
That they'd fun' on the shore at Dunoon.

The sampler his grannie had sewed at the schule,
And the pictur o' twa Hielan' kye
Wi' their feet in a loch, and ahint them a hill
An' a sun like the yolk o' an egg – hingin still
And a portrait o' grandpa forbye.

And set roun the wa' each mahogany chair
Was avoidin ilk ither ane's e'e;
For it isna the thing tae let down yere horsehair
And seat twa at a time, aye and aiblins e'en mair
Whan they rowed up the rug and pit wax on the flair
No a sicht for a paurlor tae see.

Yet owre in that corner they'd set Tammie Glen
O' melodeon players the wale;
Montgomery's Rant and the Laird o' Cockpen
Wi'' hoochin and cleekin and skirlin and then
The drouthy a' slockened they'd at it again.
Yon paurlor micht tell sic a tale.

We went owre tae the winnock and glowered at the yaird
Wi the rain drappin down frae the rone;
And it grued him the sorer the langer he started
I wad lea it again in the hour gin I dared
For there's nane o' it mine now, my faither has shared
The portion atween me and John.

And ye're welcome my fiere tae this rickle of stan
That was yours whan I gaed my ain gate;
For it's ill in the sun and it's waur in the rain,
And a' that ye'll get in the end for yere pain
Is tae live like a cuddy and die yere lea lane
In the trams o' the dungcert o' fate.

There's Erchie the orraman come frae the byre
Wi' a barra o' muck for the midden;
Erchie born in a bothie, that labours for hire,
That never has traivelled outside his ain shire,
Wha's notion o' heaven's his feet at the fire,
And juist daein ocht that he's bidden.

And then in an instant the prodigal saw
What was there in the yaird for tae see;
The ferm and the field was his brither's by law
He'd fared forth a son, but now syne his fa'
Had cam back a hired servant. Then God save us a'
But yon isna Eerchie – it's me!

Afore him the road lifted ower the brae
Till it dipped and was lost round the bend.
And he thought aince again again o' the glitterin day
Whan he first set his fit tae the rainbow way
Wi the crock fu' o' gowd at then end.

Was it wrang tae gae, was it wrang tae bide
When yere bluid's running reid in yere veins?
What's wrang wi' ambition, and what's wrang wi' pride?
When yere wants and yere wishes are dirlin inside –
Aye gin wishes were horses, then beggars wad ride,
And hae velvet tae wrap round their banes.

Whaur did my plan and my purpose gae wrang?
What sent a' my schemin aglee'
I left wi' a laugh, and I merched wi' a sang,
I never looked back and I felt ne'er a pang
My fortune I'll mak and I'll come back e'er lang
Wi' a tale that'll hae ye a' fidgin tae gang.
Was the faut in the dream, or in me?

Is this a' life offers tae auld and tae young?
Is life juist sae puir and sae sma'?
Are we orramen a' hurlin barras o' dung.
Has the laidder o' life nocht but this bottom rung?
Then why are there faur countries ava?

Sae the prodigal thocht as he stood starin owre
At the dubs and the drizzlin weet;
Nae wonder he'd sigh and nae wonder he'd glower,
At a prospect sae drear and a future sae sour,
Gruppit again by the poisening power
Whan he'd aince kenned that liberty's sweet.

Whaur was my pride? What wey did I come hame?
I was faur better aff wi' the swine.
I hadna a gigot o' veal in my wame,
My goods were a' gane and I'd nocht but my name,
Yet no' then, but now is the hour o' my shame.
Was ever heart burdened like mine.

Is it richt for a man in his need tae confess
That he isna the man he pretended?
Does a faither think mair o' his son, or think less
When his laddie comes hame juist because o' the mess
That he's made and he canna get mended.

What wad he think, that auld faither o' mine
Gin I telled him the truth this gled day,
Gin I telled him my thochts tae my hame did incline
Whan I'd nae place tae sleep there, and nae meat tae dine,
That I socht out my hame tae escape frae the swine,
There was nae ither place I could gae.

It was meat and no mercy I socht at his haun,
And a place tae lay down by puir heid.
Some dae what they wull and some dae what they maun,
Hame was bad, but at least it was better nor yon,
There was nae ither wey to get bried.

Yet he put his airms roun' me; he gied me the best
And they welcomed me hame like a king.
I'm reel weel pit on, aye I'm geyan sair dressed,
But no for the wark that I used tae detest.
The fee that ye pey for yere fling.

Noo the pairty's forgotten; ye're dune wi' the dance
And noo ye maun stump up yere fee;
It's braid daylicht noo, sae come out o' yere trance;
I'm an esquire nae mair, for I've broken my lance,
Now it's auld claes and parritch for me.

THE LAW AND THE PROFIT

THIS sermon is about a lawyer: and he doesn't show up in a very good light. So I'd better begin by describing the difference between a lawyer in Judea in Jesus' day, and a lawyer nowadays.

For one thing they didn't make nearly as much money; and for another thing, it was a different kind of law they practised. They were not allowed to make any money off practising law: so they had to make an honest living in some other way. I draw no more inferences and make no more comparisons.

They were the same people as the Scribes, and their business was more or less the same as the business of the Supreme Court in the USA. America has a written constitution: Britain does not. Which is probably one reason why America does not know where it is going, and Britain does not know where it has been.

The Founding Fathers drew up that constitution, which affirms the right of all Americans to bear arms, and whatever the President and Senate and Congress say about bearing arms, it is only the Supreme Court which can change the Constitution, as they did with the celebrated 18th amendment when America went nominally dry.

The Constitution of Jewry was the Mosaic Law: not just the Ten Commandments but all the other laws and regulations that you find, if you are interested, in Leviticus and Deuteronomy.

Whenever a new situation developed, it had to be referred to the Scribes: was this in accordance with the Mosaic law or was it not? And their word was final.

They were not at all sure of Jesus. Was his teaching constitutional, or wasn't it? And they were always trying to trap him into saying something that was not constitutional. They got him once or twice on Sabbath day regulations, but these were not all that serious. They got him finally on blasphemy. But this was a clever lawyer who thought he could lead Jesus up the garden path into an unwise statement. He learned that this is not so easy. Eternal life was the theme.

'What shall I do,' this lawyer said, 'to attain to eternal life?'

Jesus had been talking for a long time, and it was now question time. Jesus never minded questions. Any preacher knows that question time can be the most profitable time.

He put on a very simple manner, did this lawyer. He gave the impression that he was the genuine seeker. Jesus looked even more simple; even more innocent. He asked the lawyer what the law said: and the lawyer told him.

'Thou shalt love the Lord thy God with all thy heart and soul and mind and strength, and thy neighbour as thyself.' Jesus nodded approval.

'Just you do this,' he said to the lawyer, 'And eternal life is yours.' Eternal life being a way of life you live while you are alive, and not just a way of life you expect to live after you are dead.

But the catch question was still to come, and it was asked, O so innocently. 'But who is my neighbour?'

So Jesus, on the spur of the moment – and this is the genius of Jesus' parables – produced the story of the Good Samaritan. And as the story developed this scribe saw himself gradually being cornered: saw himself being engineered into a position where he would have to admit that the man who knew who his neighbour was, was not even a Jew: but a Samaritan. And the Jews hated the Samaritans. Samaria had been the capital of the northern kingdom: Israel, after Israel and Judah had split when King Solomon died. Israel fell to the Assyrians 700 years before this parable was told, and the land was populated by foreigners. Jesus knew what he was doing when he made a Samaritan the hero of his story.

And of course when he got to the end of the story, there came the straight question; 'Who was the good neighbour?'

The crowd had been lapping all this up: they could see what the punch line was going to be. And when the lawyer finally had to say, 'The Samaritan,' they enjoyed it hugely. It was very definitely one up for Jesus. The lawyer could hear them laughing at him. Jesus wasn't laughing; but Jesus was very plainly not laughing which made it all the worse.

The lawyer threshed his brain for something else to say. 'But my dear chap,' he would have loved to say, but there wasn't anything to 'but' about. He had laid a trap for Jesus and then put his own foot firmly into it. He was like the cat in Tom and Jerry who is always lighting fuses for bombs to blow up the mouse, and finding that they go off under his own tail.

And Jesus was just looking at him. Maybe his eyebrows innocently raised a little. Maybe not. But the crowd were laughing and nudging one another in the ribs with amused elbows.

The lawyer's friend took him by the sleeve and eased him away before something worse happened. What the lawyer was saying beneath his breath is not on record; but it can be left pretty well to the imagination. He muttered away and kicked stones; and then they sat down out of earshot of Jesus and the crowd, and his friend tried to refrain from saying, 'I told you so.'

'Where did I go wrong?' This was what was worrying the lawyer. Perry Mason would never have left himself open to that kind of thing. It was galling; it was maddening. In the morning it would be all over the place. He would never hold up his head again.

His friend said nothing. He thought that wiser, for the only thing he could think of saying was, 'I told you so,' and he felt that he would be risking his life, to say nothing of his friendship if he said any such thing.

Then all of a sudden the lawyer stopped gnawing his knuckles. The frown left his forehead, then came back uncertainly, then lifted again. He smiled. He slapped his thigh. He laughed. Yes, he actually laughed. He poked his friend in the ribs and he chuckled and chortled.

He had found the answer. He was a very competent lawer after all. His friend waited: not very hopefully, but he waited.

'He'll try it out on me first,' he was thinking. 'I'll tell what I think of it when I hear it. But I wish he'd forget it and let us both get home.'

'I know what you're thinking,' said the lawyer to his friend 'Accept defeat and make the best of it. He's far too clever, this Jesus chap.' His friend's face showed very clearly that the lawyer had guessed right.

'But what about the other man?' the lawyer said, and sat back and looked his friend in the eye. His friend couldn't think of any other man, and his face showed that plainly enough too.

'Come on, friend,' the lawyer coaxed confidently. 'What was the question at the end of the story?' His friend scratched his head.

'As far as I can remember,' he said, 'Jesus' question was "Which of these three, thinkest thou, was neighbour to him that fell among the thieves." ' The lawyer nodded.

'Which of these three,' he repeated. 'Why not which of these four?' And his eyes widened and the smile came back to the corners of his mouth. His friend shook his head. 'There were only three,' he said. And the lawyer laughed aloud.

'Have you forgotten the innkeeper?' And the expression on his friend's face showed clearly enough that he had forgotten the innkeeper. Not so much forgotten: the innkeeper had never as much as entered his mind. Even yet he couldn't for the life of him see what the innkeeper had to do with it. The lawyer saw this, and he explained as to a little child.

'Look friend,' he said. 'This is a story about the goodies and the baddies.' His friend nodded slowly. He still wasn't quite with it. The lawyer went on.

'The baddies are the thieves, and the priest, and the Levite. His friend nodded again. He hadn't thought about the thieves and he didn't want to say, 'And the lawyers.' In the old Jewish manner, of course.

'And the goodies?' The lawyer's eyebrows went up, and he smiled the confident smile of one who asks a question of one who doesn't know the answer. His friend scratched his head again.

'There was just the Samaritan,' he ventured. The smile became broader still.

'There was nothing of the kind, my friend. There was also the innkeeper.'

'Your father was an innkeeper?' said his friend. Just for the sake of saying something.

'Indeed he was.' The lawyer rubbed his hands. He could see the whole thing working out as Perry Mason does when he smiles yon smile at the beginning. 'The innkeeper's the professional. He gets no credit because he takes his fee. I'm the professional; I get no credit even if I take no fee. But we are the people who matter. We are still here when all thes fly-by-nights have come and gone their way. We are the people who matter. I'm going back to see this Jesus chap, and by the time I'm finished with him he'll be smiling on the other side of his face. And so will that crowd of morons who were laughing at me.'

His friend wasn't all that sure, but he couldn't think of an argument good enough to stop the lawyer. Though he felt in his heart that here was a bantam cock flying in the face of judgement. They went back down the hill. Jesus was still speaking. They waited politely.

The crowd was beginning to thin away now, for it had been a long day. They had learned a lot, but what they would remember above everything else was that story about the Samaritan and the laugh they'd had at the lawyer.

Jesus stopped, and he stretched himself. He drew his hand across his tired eyes. He yawned. He apologised to the lawyer

'I'm sorry,' he said, 'But it has been a long day. But if there is anything I can do for you, friend, I'll tire the sun with talking.' The crowd began to drift back. There was the lawyer chap again. There might be another story. There might be another laugh.

'Thank you,' said the lawyer, and he bowed. 'It was just a point I was not entirely clear about in your most interesting little story about the supposed events on the Jericho road.'

Jesus returned the bow. He sat up. He was interested.

'You said to me,' the lawyer went on, 'You said which of the three? Now shouldn't it have been which of the four?'

By the look on Jesus' face the idea had never entered his mind, but he was quick to appreciate it, and he conceded the point with a wave of his hand.

'For goodness' sake,' the lawyer's friend thought, 'he's away ahead of us again.' But it was too late to do anything with his friend except hit him over the head with something and take him away, fireman's lift.

'Could we not say . . .' And O the lawyer was so sure of himself. 'That the real neighbour was the innkeeper? Professionally, of course, he gets his fee. But no innkeeper likes injured people on the premises. It isn't good for trade. Other guests don't like it. But the innkeeper is always the man at the end of the road: the man who is left with other people's troubles. And after all, here's this Samaritan saying that he will come back and pay what's due. Can the innkeeper believe him? What if he never comes back? What if the innkeeper is left, so to speak, with the baby to hold?'

'You seem to know something about innkeepers . . .' said Jesus, gently. 'I wonder if you know as much about them as I do?'

'I should,' said the lawyer, looking round very confidently to the crowd that was crowding closer, and wishing there were more of them. 'I am an innkeeper's son.'

'Indeed,' said Jesus, gently still. He was still looking for a lead, for he could see the case the lawyer was trying to establish. The lawyer was the custodian of a tradition; the professional: while he was somebody from nowhere, like the Good Samaritan. 'Where was your father's inn?' Jesus was only trying to make time while he thought; for he was tired . . . tired.

'At Bethlehem.' And the lawyer looked round the crowd boldly. He wasn't so proud that he wouldn't admit that his father had been an innkeeper; and after all, Bethlehem was the royal town. His father should really have called Kingston Hotel, 'The Royal.' Jesus nearly smiled.

'How long ago would that be, friend?' he asked, and O, it was so guileless, the question.

'Thirty years,' said the lawyer. 'I was born in that inn.' Jesus sat up straight, and looked the lawyer straight in the eyes. 'Talking about innkeepers holding the baby,' he smiled. Sit down friend, and I'll tell you another story . . . '

THOUGHT FOR THE DAY
30th August - 3rd September, 1971

<u>MONDAY</u>

FROM time to time over the years I've broadcast portions of the bible in Scots: it's my own Scots – I pass on responsibility to nobody else. And for the week this is what we will be doing, listening to well loved verses in (my apologies to those who are not native Scots) our well loved tongue. This morning, one or two of the Psalms.

First a sad one, for this is Israel, far from home, a captive people in Babylon. It's Psalm 137 by the way.

"By the waters o' Babylon we sat sae dowff and dreary, and our e'en were wat wi' the sad, saut tear, when we thocht back on Zion.

We hangit our harps on the siller saughs that owerhung the lade.

They plaguit us sair, them that had herried us frae our hame; plaguit us sair tae sing them a sang. 'Sing us ane o' your songs o' Zion' they'd say, snickerin' awa at the sicht o' our dule.

Wae's me, how can ye tune your tongue til a sang o' Zion in a land that isna Jeshovah's?

O Jerusalem, my ain dear hame, gin ere I lichtly thee, may the skillines gae frae this right haun o' mine. Jerusalem, Jerusalem, gin ye gae frae my thochts or day oor night, lat my tongue gae dry in my mouth, gin I dinna keep ye dearest abune a' that's dear tae me."

But they came back, they came back, and they sang another song. Psalm 126.

"When the Lord brocht us back frae our thraldom tae Zion we were like folk in a dwam. We couldna believe it, and then, when it dawned on us it was true we laughed aloud and tuned our hearts til a sang.

A' roundabout the heathen bodies were sayin' ane til anither; 'Shairly the Lord maun hae dune an unco maist byordinar for them.'

Deed an he has done byordinary for us, an' weel ye may lippen tae that; and that's the wey we're sae blyth.

Will ye nae bring the lave o' them back, guid Lord, as the rain fills the burn bed birslin in the drouthy south?

Gin your heart be dowie when ye sow the seed, I warrant 'twill be lichtsome when ye win the hairst.

Your back may be bowed wi' the wecht o' the seed when ye gang out, but certes it's licht and cheery ye'll walk wi' the wecht o' the sheaves on your shouther."

Psalm 139 is the song of a man who was lost and was found.

I can nae mair win awa' frae ye Lord, then can I flee in the air. Whaur on earth can I gae tae win awa' from Thee?

Gin I sclim the verra halystead, there ye are afore me. Gin I lay me doon in the ill place; there ye are as weel.

Gin I should gae wi' the speed o' licht tae whar the lift at skreigh o' day meets the saut sea and dwal there; it wad be your ain haun that wad lead me, and your ain richt haun that wad haud me up.

Gin I should say: 'Let the mirk come doon and hap me owre, wi day nae mair and nocht but nicht about me: e'en in the howe dum deid Thou wad see me clear, and the nicht itsel' wad be bricht as the day.

Now the two best loved Psalms of all: 23 and 121.

The Lord is my hird, sae nocht sal I lack;

He faulds me i' the bughts by the haughs sae green, he gars me forrit by the lochans lown whaur he slockens my soul.

He wiseth me the road that' richt for me tae tak.

Yea, gin my gait's i' the mirk o' the glen o' the gloom o' the deid I sae fear fient a haet, for Thou art wi' me, Thy rung and Thy crummock they fend for me.

Thou plenishes my board i' the face o' my faes, Thou anointest my broo wi' the unctions o' Thy grace. My coggie's lippin' fu'.

Shairly I trow Thy bounty will aye be ahint me or I win awa', and at the hinner en" I sal bide but an' ben wi' the Lord, aye and for aye."

You'll note in the next Psalm that it's not in the hills that he finds his help. It's in the Lord.

I will lift my e'en intil the craigs.
Frae whatna airt sal come my help?

Frae the Lord sal come my help, what biggit the halystead and yirth.

He wilna let thy foot play clyte on the causey; He wilna sleep that fends for Thee. Aye, He that keeps ward on Israel sal ne'er grow dowff nor dozand.

Ye may lippen tae the Lord wha is Thy bield on the richt haun. Thou'll tak nae skaith frae the sun i' the lift, nor frae the mune i' the deid o' the nicht.

The Lord sal let nae ill come near ye; your soul He sal weird it weel. The Lord sal uphaud thee on thy road way-gaen and hame-with, frae skreigh o' day or lowsing time."

On Remembrace Day it's common to sing Psalm 124 in the second version: *"Now Israel may say."* It's a good thing to make every day remembrance day for many blessings.

Gin it hadna been that the Lord was strang for us, let Israel now say:

Gin it hadna' been the Lord was strang for us when ill-deedie men rase up again' us; they wad very near hae sweeled us leevin' when the lowe o' their wrath was bleezin' bricht.

Syne had the floods gaen owre us, the tides gaen owre our soul; syne had the waters pourin' heigh gaen swirlin' owre our soul.

Blessed be the Lord wha hasna gien us for a prey tae sic-like's teeth.

Our soul is like a bird that has slippit the girn: the girn is riven and noo we're awa' on the wing. And He that helpit us is the Lord, wha made baith the lift and the yirth.

And to end, one that is apt for many who say what the fool says: Psalm 53.

The fule has said til himsel', 'I'm shair there's nae God.'

Misleared and silly are they in their sin.

God lookit doon frae the lift upon the sons o' men tae find there's ane that kenned him; ane that socht him.

But they a' hae turned awa'; there isna ane that isna fyled. Nor ane that does guid; no' a single ane.

Hae thay a' gaen gyte, thir maisterfu' men? That destroy ither folk and think nae mair o't than takin' their dinner? And never spak' a word o' prayer in their lives?

Aye, there were God's folk, frichtened out o' their wits, and losh, there wasnae a thing tae be feared for. God had attended tae them that wad herm them.

Nae wonder they hang their heids when they see what God thinks o' them

TUESDAY

YESTERDAY we had some of the Psalms in Braid Scots. Today let's have some of the Proverbs. And the Proverbs go very well into Scots because they have the same blunt, pithy, commom sense of Scots proverbs.

We can't have them all, unfortunately, and I wouldn't even say that this is a selection of the very best of them. But here's some wise words from the first chapter, which shows that some of our problems are not as modern as we think.

Folk are always saying, "What's the world coming to?" which proves that they don't know what the world has always been.

This is advice to the young.

Gie the Lord His place and mak' a start wi' that, for it's the verry foundation o' gumption.

Anybody that lichtlies guid guiding, and thoombs his nose at what's wyce-like is just telling folk that he has nae mither-wit o' his ain,

Son, hearken til your faither, and dinna geck at what your mither bids ye.

Tak' a tellin' when ye get it, for their roid will mak' ye fit tae haud up your heid wi' anybody, and it's worth faur mair than a' the gowd in Lunnon bank.

O there's plenty will weise ye til ither airts. Just as you put them whaur they belang. Fine I ken what they'll say tae ye, for I've heard it a' mysel' in my day.

Psst, frien',' they'll whisper. 'Come on an' collogue wi' us and we'll hae a baur when the dancin' skails. We'll get our hauns on this ane an' gie him his fairin'. What does it matter gin he's dune us nae hurt? We'll dae it in the dark, doon the vennel or up a close, and suppose we kill him? The polis'll never catch us.

We'll break in here an' we'll herry them there. Ye can stash the stuff awa ablow your bed. Come in along wi' us an' we'll gie ye hackum plackum o' the hale jing bang; just the wan wallet atween us'.

Eh laddie, for ony sake hae naething ava tae dae wi' sic ill-gitted rackless diels. Dinna set fit the road they're on, for it's aye tae ill-deedidness they are ettlin', and aiblins, I wadna wonder, tae reid-wat hauns afore they're dune.

The wee bird that keeps his wits about him doesna get taingled in the net. It's the glaikit yin that's catched in the kenspeckle girn.

It's their ain bluid thir chiels are chancin'; it's nocht but their ain life they'r hazardin'.

An what's the outcome o't a' for them that's gundy-guts for the warld's gear?

A' they're daen is lain' up tribble for themsels that'll catch up wi' them in the hinner end as sure as a cat's a beast.

Chapter eight, and it's about wisdom (we'll call it "gumption") and it's as true now as it ever was.

Hear gumption cry in your lug, an' ye'll learn gin ye're gleg i' the uptak'. Heigh she stauns at the side o' the road and at the crossin'; there she is in the Gallowgate an' the Cowgate, aye, and at your ain door check. An' this is what she's sayin' tae ye.

Learn gumption ye gomeral; seek understandin' ye thowless craturs. Tak tent til what I'm tellin' ye for this is the truth aff-haun. What I'm tellin' ye's aefold, for a lee gies me the grue.

Gumption's aye dyed i' the woo, an' sooth, an' naethin' easty-wasty. Tae them that want tae see it's as plain as the nose on your face for the weel waled honest man.

The richt kennis o' gumption are faur abune siller, aye, faur abune glisterin' gowd. Owre a' the whigmaleeries men count o' muckle worth it's gumption alane that bears the gree.

C'wa' son, an' hae a rack wi' gumption hersel, for alang wi' me there aye bides canniness, and thegither we'll seek for the aefauld path that's walked by the aefauld man.

Hae respec' for the Lord and ye wilna see ill-deediness in your road. Ye'll laugh at the skeigh and the vaunty.

The man I've nae time for is the man that's twa faced.

Gin there's ony pith an' sense owre a' the yirth it's gumption. And gumption aye taks time tae think.

Gin he has gumption the king sits sure on his throne.

Gin they hae gumption the men o' law judge aricht.

I'm gumption, and I luve them that luve me. And them that seek me wi' an eident heart, they'll find me, dinna fear.

There's some that follow me, and on the road they gaither gear. They juist canna help it. There's ithers gaithe nae mair nor the respec' o' their fellow man.

Gin ye spier whilk is the better, I wad niffer a' the warld's gear for a modicul o' respec' frae my friends and faes alike.

In gumption's sicht, tae be namely for honesty when ye're leevin is better nor your laist will an' testament printed in the papers, when ye're no' there tae see it.

And this: has this a modern ring?

Thus saith the Lord. Come lookin' for me an' ye'll find what leevin's a' about. Dinna get hankit wi' your ecclesiastical dreel. There's nae profit there.

Is life worth leevin' wantin' justice – fair dealin' atween man and man?

Can the warld get anywhere wantin' richteousness?

Look up to me that hung Orion in the lift and the seven stars forebye. Look to him that brings the rising sun owre the howe dum deid o' nicht, and the gloaming and the mirk when the heat o' the day is dune and man is wearisome.

Look to him that draws the waters o' the tideless sea and draps them doon saftly on the drouthy grun'.

I'll tell ye his name . . . it is the Lord. The lord that uphauds the we man again' the big man that canna break doon his honesty.

O, I ken them; fine I ken them.

They canna put up wi' the honest chap that speaks the truth and shames the deil. I ken them; and I ken the lave o' ye forbye.

Ye're a' on the make, the hale clamjamphrey o' ye. Ye're a' for your tellies and the pub on a Friday nicht wi' the guitar bummin' awa'. But ye're in a terrible state for a' that.

An upricht man's ain guidness is bield again' ony blast; but the ill-deedie are gruppit in the girns o' their ain ill-daen. When the fell sergeant chaps at the ill-deedie man's door, that's the end o' him, and a' his houps are happit in the kirkyerd clay. But when it comes time for the aefold man tae slip awa', he gaes out frae a' the ill warld's cark and care tae his lang hame, wha'e'er comes efter him, guid or bad.

Naebody's safe frae the tongue o' a twa faced man. But the guidsense o' the godly maks him eye neeborly.

Ony toon kens the differ when he bylies are guid men and true. Ony toon can slap itsel' on the back when it's got itsel' rid o' the ither sort.

Wi' the richt man at the heid o' affairs the burgh's in good heart. Wi' ill men in chairge the toon's in a sorry state.

The man that lichtlies his neeber is daen nocht but tellin' a'body that he's nocht but a gowk himsel'. though there's plenty he micht say o' ither folk, the mensefu' man keeps his tongue atween his teeth.

Them that's aye gib-gabbin' awa' tell what's nan o' their business. But raither than gie awa' what micht hurt a body, the eident man claps his thoomb at it. There's nae guid for onybody when gumption's wi' naebody.

The poet's four wonders; and wonders they still are.

Three unce thing there be owre wonderfu' for me. Three did I say? Nae fower that I dinna ken the way o'.

The way o' the eagle in the lift; the way o' the other on the rock; the way o' a ship as she sails the saut sea; and the way o' the lad w' a lass.

Three ill things there be that mak' a tirravee. Three did I say? Nae fower that I canna be daen wi'.

An orraman made gaffer; a fule wi' a fu' wame; a flytin' woman when she's got hersel' a man; an a servant quean come intil her mistress' siller.

And some good advice about manners.

When ye're asked out for your dinner w' ane o' the knabbery, hae a guid lang look at what's set afore ye, an' gin ye're a gutsy kin o' a cratur, pit a nick in your thrapple afore ye gie wey till't.

Dinna stap yoursel' wi' the falderals for the feck o' them's but slaisters.

Dinna weary yoursel' trekin' awa' tae win siller; gie up the notion a' thegither. There's nae sense trauchlin awa for what's nae there ava'.

There's nocht can flee awa' quicker nor gear. Like an eagle spielin' in the lift, ae meenit it's there, he next it's no'.

Dinna lower yersel' tae tak' a bite o' meat frae a man wha's e'en had a glint o' greediness; nor hanker eftir the falderals that are spread on his board. A' the time he's thinkin' what it's costin' him.

"O aye" he'll say, " Rax furrit your haun an' help yirsel an' dinna haud back." But lost, man , that's nae what he's thinkin'. It' s enough tae turn your stamach owre the wee pickle you've taen. And his words wad gie ye the grue, for they're faur owre sweet tae be halesome.

Aiblins ye'll no' credit it, but there's siccan a thing as this; gi'en awa' richt royally wi' open luif, and yet hae'in mair when ye're dune.

And here's anaither thing mair common than ye'll credit; graspin and grabbin' for mair nor ye've a richt tae, and yet hae'in' less in the end o' the day.

The man that's namely for a gauchy chiel is the man wi' the open ahun'. The callan that slochens anither man's drouth will be slochened himsel' when he's drouthy.

But the man that hauds back the meal when the crops are bad and the breer is skimp, warrants the curse o' a' richt-thinkin' men. But there's naethin' but blessin' for the man that sends his corn tae market when a' body's clamourin' for it.

WEDNESDAY

ON Monday we had some of the Psalms in Scots, and yesterday morning some of the Proverbs. The trouble is that there's so much that has to be left out. But, of course, you can aye read it in the Scripture and turn it into your own Scots tongue.

Today we turn over the pages and come to the glory of the Bible: namely the Gospels. And there, again, and alas, there's so much that will have to be left out.

We could start with the story of the birth of Jesus as it's told by Matthew and Luke, bur I've done this before at Christmas time, and it's a story that goes better at Christmas, and not on a summer morning when the sun is shining. How does John start the story?

There was a man sent frae God, and John was his name. He cam' tae be witness and tae tell o' the licht, sae that a'body micht credit it through him. Himsel' he wasna the licht, he just cam' wi' the news o't. For he kenned that the licht, the true licht that lichtens ilka man in a' the wide warld, was on its way.

God was in the warld, but the warld that He had made his ane nane-sel' didna ken Him. He cam' til His ain kindrick, and it never looked the road He was on.

But now and again, an' here an' there wad be ane that would tak' Him at His word, and til' a' them that sware fealty he gied the richt tae ca' themsel's the bairns o' God Himsel'.

Sae the word becam' the tabernacle o' man, and he cam and bode wi' us. His glory was afore our verra e'en, sic glory as befits the true Son o' the true Faither, fu' o' grace and truth.

And still with John.

The verra day eftir, John was there again wi' twa o' his ain tail. He lookit straucht at Jesus as He gaed by, and says he: "Yonder gaes the Lamb o' God."

The twa o' them heard what he'd said and they went eftir Jesus. And Jesus just happened for tar turn roun' and when He saw them at his back he spiered, "What want ye wi' me, lads?"

"Maister," they say, "We were just wonderin' whaur ye bide."

"Come on and see for yoursel'," says Jesus. And the upshot was that awa' they went, and saw the place, and there they bode for the lave o' the day . . . and it was aff an and on fower in the afternune.

Ane o' the twa that heard what John had said was Andra', ain brither til Simon Peter. And what does he dae but tak' himsel' straucht aff tae Peter, and say til him, "We have fand the Saviour . . . meanin' ye'll gaither the Christ. And Andra brocht Peter to Jesus.

And a story of great faith.

In Capernaum there was a laird whase laddie was geyan far through. When they telled him that Jesus had cam' up out o' Judea and that He was in Galilee, aff he went tae see Him, and beggit Him for tae come and mak' the laddie weel that was at death's door.

Jesus says til him: "I misdoubt ye'll no' believe gin ye dinna see ferlies and uncos."

"Sir" says the laird, "Please, will ye no' come afore my laddie slips awa'."

"Awa' ye gae back hame," says Jesus, "You'll find your laddie mended and feelin' fine."

And the man lippened tae Jesus, and without anither word he turned awa'. And on the road his servants met him wi' the news. "Ye're laddie's spared. He's alive and weel."

Sae he spiered at them whaat time o' day the lad had beguid tae mend. and they telled him, "The fever went down yesterday at dinner time."

And the faither kenned that it maun hae cam' about at the verra meenit Jesus had said, "Your laddie's better."

The fourteenth of John – the most comforting chapter in Scripture.

Says Jesus: "Dinna let your heart be trauchled, ye lippen tae God, then lippen tae me, the self same way.

In my Faither's hoose, there's routh and scowth o' room. Gin it were ony ither wey, lads, I was hae tellt ye lang syne. A' I'm daen noo, is tae gang a wee afore ye and mak' your place ready for ye.

And whan I've dune that, I'll be back tae tak' ye ben mysel'. Sae ye'll aye be wi' me whaur I am. Ye ken fine whaur I'm gaen, and well ye ken the road."

Jesus says til him, "Tam, lad, I am the road, and the truth, and the life, and nae man can win near the Faither but by me."

And grim words of Jesus to those who do not serve their fellows.

Then sal he say til them on the left haun side: "Awa out o' my sicht ye ill gitted wratches, awa' tae the ill-place whaur the diel dwalls and the like o' him.

For when I was tyke-hungry did ony o' ye say, "Could ye tak' a bite o' meat?'

When I was drouthy did ye say as muckle as Collie will ye lick?"

I was lanely and nane o' ye chapped my door. When my duddies were hangin' in tatters nane o' ye thocht tae cleid me. When I was ailin' ye ne'er drapped by tae spier how I was keepin'. When I was in the jyle ye never lookit the road I was on.

Then will they spier, "Lord, never in a' our born days did we see ye famished, or drouthy, lanesome or ill-clad, ailin' or in the jyle, and dinna look efter ye."

And here's what the King will say tae them and their like. He'll say, "Ye may lippen tae this; onything ye were owre ta'en on wi' yoursels tae find time ae dae for the puirest o' my brithers, ye were owre thrang tae dae tae me."

Peter's denial, and who of us is guiltless?

But Peter followed faur ahint, or they cam' til the Heigh Priest's hoose, and he slippet intil the yaird and set himsel' doon amang the orra fowk for tae see the upshot o't a'.

And there he was when a lassie cam' by, and says she, "Here, I've seen ye afore some gait. Aye I ken whaur it was, ye were along wi' that Jesus chap."

But Peter says, "Ye're haiverin lassie. It couldna hae been me."

Sae he slippit owre closes tae the stair, and anither servin' lass got her e'en on him, and cries til them a' gaithered there: "Here's anither o' them. The cratur was wi' Jesus o' Nazareth."

"Nae me, "Peter shouts wi' an aith. "I juist dinna ken what ye're talkin' about."

But they sterted crowdin' roun' him, and first ane and syne anither says, "Aye were ye ane o' them. A blin' man could tell it by your tongue."

And Peter sterted for tae curse and sweir, and he roared, "I tell ye I dinna ken the first thing about him."

And belyve the cock crew. And a' at aince it cam' back tae Peter the word that Jesus spak til him.

"Afore cockcrow the morrow morn, ye'll hae denied me three times."

And Peter went out and gret like a bairn.

There's only one miracle of Jesus (and I think it's a miracle of sharing rather than a miracle of magic) that is in all four Gospels. We call it the feeding of the five thousand.

And as the day wore on the disciples cam' til him and said, "Here we're out at the back o' beyond, and it's wearin geyan late. Should we no' break up and let them gae and buy themselves a bite at the fairms and clachans roundabout?"

"What about attendin' tae that yoursel's," says Jesus.

"Ye mean tae sae we're tae ware a ten pun' note for breid? Is that the wey ye want us tae feed them?"

"What hae ye got in the wey o' meat?" Jesus spiers. "Awa' and hae a look."

When they cam' back they tell him, "Five scones and twa wee trouties."

Then Jesus bade the fowk sit doon in hirsels on the green grass, and they settled doon in companies o' fifty or a hunder or thereaboot. And Jesus took the five scones and the twa trouties, and liftin' up his face tae the Halydom he thankit God and brake the scones and gied them til the disciples for tae serve out tae the fowk. And he divid up the twa fish amang them a', and ilk ane ate and had his fill. Syne they gaithered up the scraps and the fish banes, and filled twal creels wi' the brock.

THURSDAY

Today, some parables.

Says Jesus: "I'll tell ye the wey they dae things in the kinrock o' God."

There was this king that went through the books tae see what servants were bethankit him.

And when he coonted up he fand that ane o' them was ten thousan' pound nae less on the wrang side. and he couldna pey his lawin'.

Sae his lord gied orders that he was tae be selled intil slaverie, and nae him alane but his wife an' his bairns and a' that he had, tae pey back what he was owin'.

But doon the mannie went on his knee banes and beggit, "Lord, but gie me anither chance an' ye'll get it a' back."

And his maister felt heart sorry for him, and says, "A' richt, I'll let ye aff for this aince."

Sae awa' went the mannie quite joco, and cam' on anither servant the same as himsel', and this ain was in his bethank for a hauf note. An' he gruppit him by the hause, and roars, "See's my siller, you."

And the chap kneeled doon and beggit him sayin' "Gie me time an' I sweir ye'll get it back."

But he wadna, and clappid him in ward tae bide there or he made it guid.

But the ither servants saw what was gaen on an' they cam' til their lord and telled him a' about it. An' he bid the first ane tae come tae see him again, and he says, "Ye ill-gittit wratch ye, I let ye aff wi'it juist for the sporin', should ye no' hae felt as sorry for your fellow as I was for yersel'?

"Sae he gied him owre tae the boot and the thumbikins, or he peyed a'that was his due. And that's what your faither in heaven will dae tae you gin affhaun and frae your heart ye dinna forgie anither ony wrang he's dune ye."

The parable of the two neighbours.

Says Jesus til them: "Suppose ye hae a frien' and he chaps on your door in the howe dum deid o'nicht and says "Auld frien', sees the len o' a puckle scones, for a frien' o' mine that has traivelled faur, has drappit in on me and I hanna a bite in the hoose tae set afore him."

And ye shout through the door, "Awa back tae your bed and dinna annoy me. The weans and me are bedded doon check for chow, and I canna get up without wakenin' them.'

I tell ye this, though ye'll no stir yoursel' for auld acquaintance sake, ye'll get up in the end for that he'll no leave the bit. Ye'll gie him a' he wants and mair juist tae see the back o' him.

An' this is what I sae tae ye; "Spier an' ye'll get what ye need. Look about ye and ye'll find what you're lookin' for. Chap the door and it'll be opened tae ye.

For ilk ane that spiers, gets; and he that looks, finds; and tae him that chaps the door is opened.

Gin ye're a faither and your laddie spiers for a piece, will ye gie him a sclate? Gin he spiers for a haddie will ye gie him an aither? Gin he wants a boiled egg will ye gie him a puddock?

Then look at it this wey. Gin you, bad and a' that ye are, ken the wey tae gie your bairns what's best for them, how muckle mair will your heavenly faither gie the Haly Speerit til them that spiers him?"

A word for the unco guid.

And Jesus telled this wee story for the guid o' the Holy Willies that think there's naebody like themsels and look doon their nobs at ither fawk.

Twa men went tae the kirk ae day; ane o' them a richt pillar, and the ither onything but. The first ane stood there and collogued wi' himself (and juist tae add a wee bit, I think Burns put what this man was thinking weel):

Yet I am here a chosen sample,
To show Thy grace is great and ample;
I'm here, a pillar o' The temple,
    Strong as a rock.
A guide, a buckler, and example
To a' Thy flock.

Wi' that digression the story gaes on. The man says tae himsel' "Twa days a week I mortify the flesh, I pay my tiends without fail. No' like yon cratur there."

And the ither, standin' awa in a corner out the road wouldna as muckle as lift his heid, but he wrung his hauns and he whispered, "Lord, I hae sinned, but will ye be kind tae me?"

I tell ye, friens, that man went hame wi 'his heart lifted, which was mair nor the ither did. For the heigher ye set yoursel', the liagher ye'll wind up. It's the man that doesna put on airs that wins to the tapmost place.

There was another humble body whom Jesus saw and used as a lesson and example.

"Watch out for the unco guid," he says til his disciples. "Them that like tae parade their Sabbath blacks, and are that pleased wi' themselves when ithers beck and bow til them, and gie them the paddit pew fornent the pulpit, and aye the tap table when they're askit out. A' the while they're sornin' on weedow women in rack-rented tenements, and coverin' it wi' mile lang prayers. I tell ye what will happen tae that sort: they'll wind up in the ill place."

And he lookit up and saw a' the bien folk drappin their collections in the plate, and his e'e fell on a weedow woman slippin' in twa bawbees. Says he, "Ye may lippen tae this, that puir body has put in more than them a' . They've gien what they could weel dae without, but she, for a' her poortith, has gien the last maik in her spung."

It was the fast day, and John's disciples and the ithers were haudin' the fast. They cam' tae Jesus and they spier: "What wey dae them that follow John haud the fast and your friens dinna?"

Says Jesus; "Ye dinna expec' your friens at the weddin' tae be glum when the bridesman's wi them, dae ye?"

"There'll come a day when he's taen awa' and that will be time enouch tae be dowie."

He went on, "Shairly naebody in his sicht mind wad shew a clout o' unshrunk claith on an auld coat. Gin he did, the new wad tear the auld and the hole wad be waur nor it was afore. Naebody puts new wine in an auld skin; gin ye did the wine wad burst it, and ye'd tyne baith the blaither and the bree. Na, na, friens. New blaithers for new wine.

Later on they sent some o' the Pharisees, and some o' them were a' for Herod, tae try for tae inveigle him intil a colliebuction.

They cam' forrit and say til him, "Maister, we ken you're an aefuald man and that ye dinna gie a thocht what folk think o' ye. It's plain enouch ye're nae lackin' for a clap on the back frae onybody, but teach the weys o' God, haudin leal tae the truth. Tell us, is it richt tae pey taxes tae Caesar? Are we tae pey or are we no'."

But Jesus saw through them a' richt. Says he, "Ye wadna offer tae tak' a len' o' me wad ye? Hae ye a plack in your sprung? See's a look at it." So they brocht ane.

"Noo, wha's face wad this be?" he spiers, "And wha's name an' title wad this be?"

"It's Ceasars," they say. And Jesus went on, "Then juist ye gie til Caesar what belangs tae Caesar, and gie tae God what belangs tae God."

And they didna ken whaur tae look.

FRIDAY

THE story teller was and still is a feature of bazaar and market in the east, and Jesus was a great story teller. He was always sure of an audience, and he took good advantage of it, for all his stories have a point. None more so than this one.

Aince there was a man that had twa sons, and ae day the younger loon says til his faither, "Dad, I want what's mine o' the haudin, graith, gear an' bestial."

Sae the fairmer thocht nae herm and he portioned it out, hackum plackum, and nae lang eftir the young chap gaithered a' the siller he'd got, and aff he went quite joco for tae see the world. And he put the hale jing bang owre the buss taps, fetch and fill mair, or he hadna a tinker's tippence.

But there was mair ill tae come. For there cam' on the land an almichty dearth, and he didna ken whaur tae turn next.

Sae he fee'd himsel' til a fairmer in thir pairts and he sent him doon the holme tae bayte the swine.

And he ettled tae fill his wame wi' the brock, and nae man said "Have ye a mooth?"

And sittin' there he tocht til himsel' "What on earth am I daen' here, near deid for want o' bite and sup, and at hame there's nae a halflin aboot the place that hasna a' the meat he can haud and mair."

"I'll haud awa' hame tae my dad, and I'll say til him, "Dad, I've made an unco mess o't. I've wrangit heaven and I've wrankit yoursel, and I'm nae mair fit tae be kent a your son. Will ye fee me for your orraman?"

Sae awa' he went, and faur, faur doon the road his old faither saw him, and ran and put his erms aboot his neck and bussed him, he was that wae for him.

And the loon said what he'd made up his mind tae say, "Dad I hae wrangit heaven and I've wrangit yoursel', I'm nae mair fit tae be kent as your son."

But the faither cries til them a' roundabout, "Get thir duddies aff him and busk him in braws, a ring on his haun and shoes on his puir feet. Bring out the prize beast and kill it, for we've a nicht afore us, friens. For here's my laddie that I thocht was deid, and he's leevin'; here's my son that was tyned and I've fand him again."

So they a' yokit tae for the time o' their lives.

But the aulder son was at the plooin', and when he was lowsed he cam' roun' the rigg, and he heard the fiddlin' an the hoochin'. Sae he ca'ed ower the cattleman and spiers at him whit's a' the commotion.

And he says, "It's that your brither's cam' hame, and your faither's bid us a' til a pairty for that he's got him back safe and sound."

But he was took the stordies and wouldna gang in; sae his faither cam' out and begged him.

But he said til his faither, "See here, dad, a' my life hae I dune your biddin', and ne'er put my left foot where my richt foot should be, and ye never as muckle as gied me a hen for me tae hae a nicht wi' my friens; but nae sooner does he come hame that's wasted a' his siller wi' the kitties, ye put out the best afore him."

And his faither says til him, "Laddie ye're wi' me a' the time and a' that I hae is your ain. Shairly it was but richt we should hae a splore, for it's your brither, and he was died tae us, and now he's leevin' again; we thocht he was tyned for aye, but we've fand him again."

And this other old, familiar story which is always new.

There was this lawyer chap that got up and tried for tae bamboozle Jesus.

"Maister" he says, "What maun I dae for tae win eternal life?"

"What does the law lay down," says Jesus. "How div ye read it yoursel'?"

The man says, naethin' laith, "Ye maun lo'e the Lord w' a' your heart and wi' a' your soul and wi' a' your micht and wi' a' your mind . . . and your neebor as yoursel'."

And Jesus says, "Richt ye are, frien' and that's the hale hypothic. Juist you dae that and a' will be weel wi' ye."

But this wassna what the lawyer was eftir, so he spiers, "But wha is my neebor?"

Jesus says, "There was this man that was traivellin' doon the road frae Jerusalem tae Jericho, and a gang o' caterans fell on him. They strippet the duddies aff him and gied him an unco hammerin', and ran awa leavin' him hauf deid. And eftir a wee, ane o' the rulin' elders cam' alang, but when he saw the man lyin' he crossed owre and went by.

And anither ane, and douce and respectable he was, cam' by and took ae look at the mannie, and he crossed the road and went on his way.

But there was the Samaritan on his traivels, and when he saw him he was heart sorry for him, and cam' owre and bandaged him up, and wipit his hurts wi' ile and a drap o' speerits, and he got him up on his garron and brocht him til an inn and lookit efter him a' that night.

And on the morn afore he set aff again he took out twa hauf croons and he gied them til the innkeeper and says til him, "Look eftir him, will ye, and gin it costs ye ony mair I'll mak' it up to ye when I come this way again."

"Now, frien'," says Jesus, "Out o' thir three, whilk, div ye think, was neebor tae the man that fell in wi' the rievers?"

And the lawyer said, "The man that did somethin' for him."

"Richt ye are," says Jesus. "Sae a' ye need is tae gang and dae the same yoursel'."

We're all pretty good with excuses for not doing what we don't want to do, and if we're good enough at excuses we can repeat them so often that they become reasons. Jesus has a word for us.

And ane that was listening to Jesus at the dinner says til him when they had cleared the table, "Wad it no' be grand tae draw your chair into the table o' the kinrock o' God."

And the maister started aff again.

"There was this man," he says "That made up his mind tae hae a maist byordnar dinner pairty, and he askit dizzens o' his friens and neebors tae come. And juist tae mak' siccar they didna' forget he sent a man rou' the doors tae mind them it was on that nicht."

And ane eftir the ither they a' beguid for tae say what wey they couldna manage.

This ane says, "I've juist bocht a field o' tatties and I'll need for tae gang and see gin they're fillin' out. Tell your maister I'm real sorry."

And anither says, "I've juist bocht mesel' five pairs o' horse and I haena seen them workin' yet. Tell your maister that I'm that upset for that I canna come."

And a third ane says, "I've juist got mysel' married and the wif'll no' let me out o' her sicht. I'm shair your maister will understaun'."

Sae the man cam' hame and told his maister and he was neither tae haud norbind.

"Awa ye go ootbye," says he, "And gae roun' the toon and dinna come back or ye've a' the puir bodies, and the lame and the blin' folk."

And the servant did as he was bid and cam' back and said there was still a place or twa. Says the maister, "Look in the vennels and closes and back greens and mak' them come in. I want tae see my hoose filled. For I'll tell ye this and tell ye nae mair, that nane o' them I askit first will taste a spunefu' o' my meat."